Adorning Maitreya's Intent

Adorning Maitreya's Intent

Arriving at the View of Nonduality

ༀ༎དབུས་དང་མཐའ་རྣམ་པར་འབྱེད་པའི་

རྣམ་པར་བཤད་པ་མི་ཕམ་དགོངས་རྒྱན༎

Rongtön Sheja Künrig

TRANSLATED BY
Christian Bernert

FOREWORDS BY
*H.H. Sakya Trizin and
Khenpo Ngawang Jorden*

SNOW LION
BOULDER
2017

Snow Lion
An imprint of Shambhala Publications, Inc.
4720 Walnut Street
Boulder, Colorado 80301
www.shambhala.com

9 8 7 6 5 4 3 2 1

First edition

Printed in the United States of America

♾ This edition is printed on acid-free paper that meets the
American National Standards Institute Z39.48 Standard.
♻ This book is printed on 30% postconsumer recycled paper.
For more information please visit www.shambhala.com.

Distributed in the United States by Penguin Random House LLC
and in Canada by Random House of Canada Ltd

LIBRARY OF CONGRESS CATALOGING-IN-PUBLICATION DATA
Names: Rong-ston Shes-bya-kun-rig, 1367–1449, author. | Bernert,
    Christian, translator.
Title: Adorning Maitreya's intent: Arriving at the View of Nonduality /
    Rongtön Sheja Künrig; translated by Christian Bernert.
Other titles: Dbus dang mtha' rnam par 'byed pa'i rnam bshad mi pham
    dgongs rgyan. English
Description: Boulder: Snow Lion, 2017. | Includes bibliographical
    references and index. | Includes translation from Tibetan.
Identifiers: LCCN 2016011616 | ISBN 9781611803662 (paperback: alk. paper)
Subjects: LCSH: Maitreyanātha Madhyāntavibhaṅga. | Yogācāra
    (Buddhism)—Early works to 1800. | BISAC: RELIGION / Buddhism /
    Tibetan. | RELIGION / Buddhism / Sacred Writings.
Classification: LCC BQ2965 .R6813 2017 | DDC 294.3/85—dc23
LC record available at https://lccn.loc.gov/2016011616

CONTENTS

FOREWORD

I am very pleased that Rongtön Sheja Künrig's unsurpassable commentary on Maitreya's *Madhyāntavibhāga* has been translated into English and thus made available to a great number of Dharma students worldwide.

Founder of Nalendra Monastery in Tibet and one of the foremost exponents of the Yogācāra school of thought, Rongtön Sheja Künrig is known as one of the "Six Ornaments of Tibet." A formidable scholar and a mystic, he is regarded as an emanation of Maitreya as well as a reincarnation of some of the greatest Indian *panditas* of the past.

In this masterful work, Rongtön Sheja Künrig elucidates with remarkable clarity the core teaching contained in the *Madhyāntavibhāga*, describing in detail the process of liberation from a state of total affliction to the realization of the inseparability of clarity and emptiness.

Christian Bernert's translation, *Adorning Maitreya's Intent: Arriving at the View of Nonduality*, aptly conveys the essence of the great Sakya master's treatise, while making it accessible to those readers who lack advanced philosophical training. It is bound to greatly deepen the understanding of all who undertake its study and it will surely be a source of great benefit to all.

The Sakya Trizin
October 5, 2016

Foreword

Awakened wisdom is known to be both vast and profound, allowing an enlightened being to teach others according to their dispositions. Countless masters have studied, contemplated, and meditated on the Buddha's words and have attained freedom from delusion as a result of their efforts. Many have commented on his words, guiding later generations to the same realizations. Based on their realization, on the perspective they adopted to teach the Dharma, and on the receptivity of their audience, the teachings developed in various ways, giving rise to the diverse traditions of Buddhism we know today.

We are extremely pleased to publish the translation of an important commentary on the *Madhyāntavibhāga,* a key treatise for the understanding of the Yogācāra tradition, one of the main systems of Buddhist thought and practice in India. Composed by the great Sakya scholar Rongtön Sheja Künrig (1367–1449), this commentary elucidates crucial concepts of the tradition, like a key unlocking the door of an immeasurable treasury.

By the merit generated with this work, may all beings realize that which lies beyond duality.

With my best wishes,

Khenpo Ngawang Jorden
Director of the International Buddhist Academy (IBA)
Kathmandu, Nepal
March 2016

ACKNOWLEDGMENTS

Of the many individuals who contributed to the production of this book, we would like to extend our thanks in particular to Khenpo Jamyang Kunga, a direct disciple of the late Khenchen Appey Rinpoche, who taught this text to the translator over a one-month period in Kathmandu in the autumn of 2012. We also thank Ven. Ngawang Tenzin from the International Buddhist Academy, Kathmandu, who took the time to read through the entire text along with the manuscript of the translation. Thanks are due also to the Venerable French monk Damien Jampa for reviewing the work, to Vivian Paganuzzi for editing and proofreading, and to Markus Viehbeck and Rory Lindsay for their suggestions for the introduction.

We would also like to thank Nikko Odiseos and the entire Shambhala team for taking on this project and assisting us throughout the last stages of publication.

Finally, we would like to express our gratitude to the Khenchen Appey Foundation for funding this project.

ADORNING MAITREYA'S INTENT

Translator's Introduction

The Buddhist Path

Buddhism is often referred to as the *Middle Way*, a path free of extremes. As a seeker, Siddhartha Gautama recognized the futility of a worldly life indulging in sense pleasures, and also the inefficacy of extreme forms of spiritual practice, and decided to renounce both. As the Buddha, the Awakened One, he realized that all mistaken views are contained within the extremes of permanence and annihilation, and taught a view free of speculative assertions about reality.

The path taught by the Buddha is based on a profound understanding of reality, and by following it one is led to realize the way things really are, free from mental projection and personal interpretation, without adding to or denying any aspect of the actual state of things. It is this insight that will free the individual from the delusion that is at the very root of all suffering.

Not understanding the real nature of experience, beings are entangled in all sorts of conflicting views and become emotionally unbalanced, generating aversion to certain experiences and attachment to others. This steers the mind away from the peace that is its ultimate nature. The Buddhist path is like a tool to unmask the distorted views we hold and the unwholesome conduct that ensues from those views. Fundamentally a wisdom (*prajñā; shes rab*)–oriented tradition, its foundation consists of establishing ethically sound discipline (*śīla; tshul khrims*) and cultivating wholesome forms of concentration (*samādhi; ting nge 'dzin*).

According to Buddhist tradition, wisdom is developed by first studying the teachings, then analyzing them, and finally cultivating in meditation the profound understanding gained through study and analysis. Scholars and practitioners of the past have composed a great many treatises commenting on the words of the Buddha and his disciples, providing us with many ways to analyze and deeply understand the nature of reality.

THE ROLE OF BUDDHIST PHILOSOPHY

In the scriptures, Buddha Shakyamuni is often depicted as a very practical person, sometimes actively discouraging his followers from engaging in speculative arguments. In the *Cūla-Mālunkyovada Sutta*, for instance, in the parable of the poisoned arrow, the Buddha tells a disciple that metaphysical speculation can be a dangerous waste of time by likening it to a soldier wounded by a poisoned arrow who refuses to be treated until he knows everything about the arrow and the soldier who shot it.[1] Instead, we are encouraged to *do something* about the suffering we experience and its causes by following the path he laid out.

Why, then, one might reasonably ask, has the tradition produced this gigantic collection of writings of a philosophical nature? Of course, that depends on what we mean by philosophy in the first place. However we may choose to define it, in the context of the Buddhist tradition, philosophical argumentation has a soteriological function. It is an aid to liberation designed to remove confusion about the path and reality itself.

An important concept in this regard is that of "view" (*dṛṣṭi*; *lta ba*), featured in various lists condensing the Buddhist path into its key elements.[2] It refers to a correct understanding of the world and of the path to liberation, and thus forms the basis for one's meditative training and conduct in daily life. Without the right view one is said to be like a blind person, unable to see where one is headed and incapable of avoiding obstacles on the way. With the right view, however, one will be able to distinguish wholesome from unwholesome, true from false, and will then be able to progress on the path. By cultivating and refining the right view, one is able to shed increasingly subtle veils of ignorance (*āvaraṇa; sgrib pa*), making the mind increasingly free. It is thus the view that will determine to what degree an individual is bound in perpetual cycles of suffering and dissatisfaction (i.e., samsara) or is free from conditioned existence (i.e., nirvana). The highest view is one that perfectly understands phenomena in terms of both their ultimate nature (*ji lta ba mkhyen pa*) and their conventional existence (*ji snyed pa mkhyen pa*), and is a quality exclusive to buddhas. In this sense, the right view represents not only the foundation but also the means and the aim of the path.

The role of Buddhist dialectics is simply to establish the "right view," correctly and beyond doubt, either for oneself or for others. What is the right view precisely? How does one know whether one's understanding is accurate or mistaken? How does one refute wrong views about reality and prove to others that one's own understanding is the right one? It is the answers to these questions that mushroomed into the vast libraries of what we might call Buddhist philosophy.

THE THREE TURNINGS OF THE DHARMA WHEEL

It is said that the Buddha's method of guiding his followers was always adapted to his audience. His teaching is likened to the way specific medicines are used to cure particular diseases. Thus the instructions given to a certain group of disciples in a given context were not in line with—or even seemed to contradict—teachings given at another time, simply because it was not appropriate for all students to hear the same words in order to progress on the spiritual path.

To help later followers distinguish between the words that are to be taken literally and those that require interpretation, the *Saṃdhinirmocanasūtra* (*Sutra Unraveling the Intent*) introduces the hermeneutic principle of differentiating between interpretive meaning (*neyārtha; drang don*) and definitive meaning (*nītārtha; nges don*). With this tool, the discourses may be divided into three groups called *turnings*. The first two turnings are interpretive and the third one is definitive, according to this sutra.

In the sutras of the first turning based on the exposition of the four *ārya* truths,[3] the Buddha affirms the existence of certain phenomena such as form, feeling, discrimination, formative factors, and consciousness, that is, the five *skandhas,* or psychophysical groups of phenomena that make up a human being. What is denied in those discourses is the existence of an independent, substantially existent identity or self, which is asserted to be imputed on the basis of those skandhas.

In the sutras of the second turning based on the Perfection of Wisdom (*prajñāpāramitā*) teachings, the existence of these phenomena is denied. In the discourses of this group we find words such as, "no form, no feeling, no discrimination, no formative factors, no consciousness," and so forth. These passages refer to the emptiness (*śūnyatā; stong pa nyid*) or lack of inherent existence of all phenomena, explained to be their ultimate reality.

To resolve the contradictions emerging from the first two turnings, the Buddha turned the Dharma wheel a third time, making a clear distinction between the discourses of interpretive meaning and those of definitive meaning. In these teachings, certain phenomena are identified as nonexistent, while others are defined as bearing the characteristics of existence. The emphasis in this group of discourses is on the luminous and primordially untainted nature of mind, the potential for awakening, or buddha-nature, present in all beings, and on the three-nature model of reality that will be explained below. The *Sutra Unraveling the Intent* is itself part of this group.

THE YOGĀCĀRA TRADITION

Over time, a number of Buddhist schools of thought emerged in India, adhering to the various ideas presented in the sutras. The two main Mahayana schools of thought, Madhyamaka and Yogācāra, are related to the second and third turnings of the Dharma wheel respectively.

Based on the Perfection of Wisdom sutras and the writings of the Indian master Nāgārjuna (fl. 2nd century C.E.), the Middle Way school (*madhyamaka; dbu ma*) emphasizes the doctrine of emptiness, that is, the lack of self-nature asserted to be the ultimate reality of all phenomena. The Yogācāra tradition evolved based on the sutras of the third turning, such as the *Saṃdhinirmocana* and the *Laṅkāvatāra,* and the writings of Asaṅga (fl. 4th century C.E.).[4]

The Yogācāra tradition is known by various names, depending on which aspects of its teachings are stressed. When the emphasis is on the importance of meditation and spiritual discipline, it is called the School of the Practice of Yoga (*yogācāra; rnal 'byor spyod pa*). When its philosophical emphasis is on the mind's role in creating the reality we experience, it is called the Mind Only (*cittamātra*) school, Cognition Only (*vijñaptimātra*) school, or the School of Consciousness (*vijñānavāda*).

Scriptural Sources[5]

The following sutras are considered to be among the main canonical sources of the Yogācāra tradition: *Saṃdhinirmocanasūtra* (*Sutra Unraveling the Intent*), *Laṅkāvatārasūtra* (*Sutra on the Descent to Lanka*), *Avataṃsaka-sūtra* (*Flower Ornament Sutra*), and *Samādhirājasūtra* (*King of Samadhi Sutra*). With varying emphasis, these scriptures teach notions such as the three natures or the all-base consciousness, which are the cornerstones of Yogācāra philosophy.

In addition to the canonical scriptures, the following Indian treatises (*śāstra; bstan bcos*) are considered fundamental to the development of Yogācāra thought: Maitreya's *Mahāyānasūtrālaṃkāra* (*Ornament to the*

Mahayana Sutras), *Madhyāntavibhāga* (*Distinguishing the Middle from the Extremes*), and *Dharmadharmatāvibhāga* (*Distinguishing Dharmas from their True Nature*); Asaṅga's *Yogācārabhūmiśāstra* (*Treatise on the Grounds of Yogācāra*) and *Abhidharmasamuccaya* (*Abhidharma Compendium*); and Vasubandhu's *Viṃśatikākārikā* (*Twenty Stanzas*) and *Triṃśikākārikā* (*Thirty Stanzas*).

This work will not provide details on the contents of these scriptures. Suffice it to say, these texts contain a wealth of ideas that would lead to the transformation and development of Buddhist thought in India and beyond.

Fundamental Concepts

To get a general understanding of this tradition it will be helpful to consider some of its most fundamental concepts. Three of the most important are (1) the idea that what we experience is only mind or mental representation (*cittamātra/vijñaptimātra*), (2) the *ālayavijñāna* or all-base consciousness, and (3) the three-nature model of reality (*trisvabhāva*). It is important, however, not to reduce Yogācāra to merely these concepts, which, if isolated from the basic Buddhist framework, might lead to a misrepresentation of the tradition. As Brunnhölzl points out, Yogācāra is a vast, complex, and complete system of Buddhist thought and practice rooted in the sutras.[6] It covers the entire spectrum of Buddhist philosophy, from the Abhidharma categories of mind and matter to the *pramāṇa* methods of epistemology and the Madhyamaka concept of emptiness, which, as we will see, is interpreted in a new light. Yogācāra also discusses the process of the purification of mind on the most subtle levels, mapping out the inner journey of mental cultivation in unprecedented detail. The categories singled out below were selected to highlight certain aspects of this tradition to help us appreciate its unique contributions to the development of Buddhist thought in India.

Mind Only

It is generally asserted in all Buddhist traditions that an understanding of the mind is of central importance in our quest to resolve the problems of existence at their root. In the Yogācāra tradition, a particular emphasis is placed on the role of the mind in creating a world of confusion and suffering. Statements by the Buddha such as "the three realms are mind only" and similar passages are found in a number of Mahayana sutras.[7]

According to D'Amato, two Buddhist doctrines are important to consider as precursors to the idea of "representation only": the doctrine of momentariness (*kṣaṇikatva*; *skad cig ma nyid*) and that of signlessness (*ānimitta*; *mtshan ma med pa*).[8] Momentariness refers to the idea that phenomena are in a subtle but constant state of change; things exist for a single moment and instantly pass away. As long as causes and conditions are similar, the resulting phenomenon will have a similar appearance (similar, but not identical, since the causes and conditions needed for the production of a given thing are themselves also in a state of flux). This momentary nature thus accounts for the fact that things eventually grow old in a way that is perceptible to the naked eye. Generally when relating to phenomena, however, we do not directly perceive the reality of subtle impermanence. What we relate to is the mental image of those objects formed in the mind, the mere cognition or representation (*vijñapti*; *rnam rig*) of things, which we then identify as the objects themselves. In a way, we could say that the world we live in is like ever-flowing water, but the world we think in is like a frozen image. Meditation techniques such as the close applications of mindfulness (*smṛtyupasthāna*; *dran pa nyer gzhag*) are used to counteract such mistaken perceptions of the world.

In an influential article, Lambert Schmithausen argues that several exclusively Buddhist theories have their roots in experiences brought about by spiritual practice, rather than by theoretical speculation.[9] One of the theories he discusses is that of representation only as presented in the *Saṃdhinirmocanasūtra*, the earliest canonical scripture to explicitly discuss the question of the nonexistence of external objects. In this text, it is affirmed not only that imagined objects generated in meditation are unreal in the sense of not existing separately from the mind, but that all objects of perception are similarly representation only.[10]

Discussions of the controversial nature of such statements abound in both traditional and modern scholarship. Did the Buddha merely emphasize the importance of the mind in our experience of the world and its transcendence, or did he actually mean that there are no external objects "out there," that there is only one reality, namely *mind*?

If this teaching is really of a phenomenological nature (meaning that it is not concerned with things but with the *experience of things*), then the question of whether or not there is a world "out there" becomes secondary. The main purport of this teaching would gravitate toward the only plane of existence accessible by the mind, namely the world *as it is received* (as opposed to the world *as it is*). This approach is particularly relevant from a soteriological perspective. The world as it is reflected in consciousness is the place where suffering is experienced, nowhere else. This is also where suffering ceases.

All-Base Consciousness[11]

Another fundamental concept in Yogācāra is the existence of eight types of consciousness, which expands on the traditional model of the six consciousnesses based on the six sense faculties. The two additional aspects of consciousness are the all-base consciousness (*ālayavijñāna; kun gzhi rnam shes*) and the afflicted mind (*kliṣṭamanas; nyon mongs pa can gyi yid*), two subtle levels of awareness not obvious to ordinary perception. The *all-base* is the fundamental, underlying structure of experience, the uninterrupted flow of the mental continuum. The mind that focuses on the all-base, identifying its subtle continuum as the self, is termed the *afflicted mind*.

While the six sense consciousnesses constantly change objects and are even suspended during certain states (such as deep sleep, coma, or special states of meditative absorption), the all-base flows steadily in an uninterrupted stream. Without the existence of this consciousness, it would be difficult to account for the continuity of experience, rebirth, and the maturation of karma in either the distant future or a future life. If all consciousness comes to a stop in deep sleep or in the state of temporary cessation (i.e., a state of meditative absorption in which all consciousness and mental activity is suspended), what is the cause for its reemergence once the individual comes out of these states?[12] And what is the link between an action carried out in the past and its karmic result in the future? According to Yogācāra, it is the all-base consciousness that enables this process.

It is termed "basis of all" because as the source of the other seven consciousnesses, it is the foundation of all experience. One of its main functions is as a "storehouse," containing the seeds (*bīja; sa bon*) and latencies (*vāsanā; bag chags*) of all actions. Every karma, every deed of body, speech, and mind, leaves a mark or imprint on the most subtle mental continuum. These imprints are like seeds in the sense that they contain the potential for a future experience that will be of the same nature as the action that produced it (i.e., wholesome seeds will produce pleasant experiences and unwholesome seeds unpleasant ones). In this way, they function as latencies conditioning the mind to experience a world of its own making, the appearance of which depends on the quality of the mental factors prevalent at the time of the action.

The all-base has two aspects: a causal aspect composed of seeds and latencies; and a resultant one that is the all-base itself, the support the seeds are placed in. They are just two sides of the same coin. One aspect of this fundamental consciousness is its karmic contents (i.e., the seeds and latencies) taken individually, and the other is its continuum, which functions as the repository for further imprints.

Neutral in nature, the all-base accommodates all types of seeds equally, whether they are wholesome, unwholesome, or neutral. It therefore merely stores the latencies, without itself ever being tainted by the afflictions. In this way, it functions as a basis not only for samsaric experience but for nirvana as well.

Three Natures and the Path

We now come to the third basic principle of the Yogācāra tradition, that of the three natures. This triad is of central importance as it represents both a model of reality (equivalent to that of the two realities of Madhyamaka) and a description of the Yogācāra path to enlightenment.

All phenomena are said to be composed of the three natures: the imputed (*parikalpita; kun brtags*), the dependent (*paratantra; gzhan dbang*), and the perfected (*pariniṣpanna; yongs grub*). These three represent distinct aspects of the same realities, different in appearance but inseparable in nature.

It is a fundamental principle of Buddhism that all phenomena arise due to causes and conditions. There is no intrinsic nature to things, only dependent arising. In Yogācāra, the cause for experience of any kind is not to be found somewhere outside—it is the latencies produced by past actions left on the all-base consciousness. Objects perceived as external to consciousness induce the experience of pleasant, unpleasant, or neutral sensations. These "objects," however, are nothing but the maturation of the mind's own latencies appearing as objects. The counterpart of these apprehended objects is the mind apprehending them, both originating from the same seed.

In this way, we have seeds that are produced in dependence on causes and conditions, and the imagination of the unreal (*abhūta-parikalpa; yang dag ma yin pa'i kun tu rtog pa*), which consists of the erroneous conception that objects and the mind are separate, independent entities. These are the first two natures: the imputed, which is dualistic perception, the erroneously imputed existence of apprehended objects and the apprehending mind; and the dependent, which refers to the nature of experience and phenomena, arising in dependence on causes and conditions. The third nature, then, is the perfected. It is the realization of the true nature of appearances. In other words, it is the understanding that in reality the dependent nature is devoid of the imputed existence of the dual entities of apprehended and apprehender. Realizing the nonexistence of this duality is the realization of emptiness according to Yogācāra.

To reiterate, the imputed nature is false, as the dualistic view of apprehended and apprehender is a mistaken perception of reality. The fact remains, however, that the deluded mind has these dualistic appearances. This is the dependent nature, including all appearances, which are nothing but the manifestations of the latencies placed on the all-base and which become manifest based on causes and conditions. The dependent nature is said to exist in the sense that it functions as the basis for confusion. The perfected nature consists of the realization that the duality of apprehended and apprehender is imagination of the unreal, and of its real nature, suchness (*tathatā; de bzhin nyid*).

D'Amato speaks of two ways of understanding the three natures, which he calls the pivotal and the progressive models.[13] According to the first one, the imputed and the perfected natures are two ways of seeing the dependent nature. A mind under the influence of ignorance sees a dualistic world divided into apprehended objects and the apprehending mind. This imagination of the unreal produces a mistaken view of reality, which is called the imputed. When the mind is free of the erroneous projection of duality (based on the latencies), it becomes aware of the dependent nature of experience (produced by the mind itself). This is called the perfected. The imputed and the perfected thus represent a fundamental shift of perspective, a shift brought about by ridding the all-base of all contaminated seeds. Since the seeds and the all-base are two sides of the same entity, there is no all-base without seeds. When this purification is attained, it is called the transformation of the basis (*āśrayaparāvṛtti; gnas yongs su 'gyur ba*).

According to the progressive model, the three natures represent progressively more profound views of reality. A mind deluded by the appearance of things only sees the imputed. A mind trained in correct analysis and meditation understands the dependent nature of appearances. And a mind fully trained in this way has purified all latencies of duality along with their traces and has attained the transformation of the basis, which coincides with a perfect nonconceptual view of suchness, the ultimate. This is the perfected.

According to D'Amato, the *Madhyāntavibhāga* mainly teaches the pivotal model of the three natures.

Yogācāra in Tibet

In Tibetan doxography (*grub mtha'*), the Indian Buddhist schools of thought are often presented in a hierarchical order, beginning with the realist schools of Vaibhāṣika and Sautrāntika, followed by Cittamātra, and culminating in the Madhyamaka view. In this way, Mind Only is often seen as inferior to the school of the Middle Way based on Nāgārjuna's treatises. From the perspective of the proponents of this last tradition, all the other schools fall into the extreme of permanence, clinging to the idea of "existence" in one way or another. Only Madhyamaka, they say, teaches the genuine Middle Way free from all conceptual elaborations, making it untenable for anyone to adhere to any of the lower systems.[14]

But not all scholars made such clear-cut distinctions between the schools. Yogācāra did have a great influence on a number of scholars and traditions. From the early days of Buddhism in Tibet, Yogācāra had its supporters in the Land of Snows. In particular, the celebrated Indian abbot Śāntarakṣita (725–788) brought Yogācāra-Madhyamaka to Tibet, and was responsible for introducing the monastic and scholastic lineages there as well. This system represents a kind of synthesis of both schools, using the Mind Only view to explain the conventional level of reality, and the emptiness of the Middle Way to explain the ultimate level.[15] It is true however, that even though masters like Śāntarakṣita had integrated the Yogācāra view into their systems, they were principally upholders of Madhyamaka. The final philosophical message imported to Tibet was thus the understanding of emptiness according to the Middle Way, and this is the tradition that was given priority in terms of study and exposition.

Later indigenous Tibetan masters close to the Yogācāra school include the third Karmapa Rangjung Dorje (1284–1339); Dolpopa Sherab Gyaltsen (1292–1361) and Jetsün Taranatha (1575–1634), both related to the Jonang tradition; Shakya Chokden (1428–1507) from the Sakya tradition; and two masters of the nineteenth century who were instrumental in the nonsectarian Rimé movement, Jamgön Kongtrul (1813–1899) and Ju Mipham (1846–1912). The register of terms and imagery used in the writings of these masters is very close to that found in the Yogācāra treatises. What these masters hold in common is an association with a label that remains controversial to the present day: "zhentong" (*gzhan stong;* "other-emptiness"). This term is used to denote a subschool of Madhyamaka. The tenets of this school affirm that mind is devoid of afflictions and stains, which are not inherent to its nature, but is not empty of its innate enlightened qualities, which only become manifest upon the attainment of awakening. The term "zhentong" is used in contrast to "rangtong" (*rang stong;* "self-emptiness"), which refers to the school that adheres to the views of Nāgārjuna's brand of Madhyamaka, which asserts that all phenomena, including the mind, are empty of self-nature. However, it would be a mistake to think that the views of these masters are identical. Each of them developed his own system, which accounts for the beauty and diversity in the rich philosophical heritage of Tibetan Buddhism.[16]

Dolpopa Sherab Gyaltsen was an early Tibetan defender of the Cittamātra system, arguing that the teachings expressed in the third turning of the Dharma wheel and expounded by the "vast activity lineage" of Maitreya and Asaṅga were in no way inferior to the "profound view" taught by Nāgārjuna. Distinguishing between a conventional and an ultimate Cittamātra, Dolpopa identified the latter as the actual teachings of Maitreya and Asaṅga, which he includes in the "Great Madhyamaka" tradition.[17]

Shakya Chokden developed one of the most sophisticated alternatives to the standard fourfold model of the Indian schools of thought, based on his understanding of subtle aspects of the Yogācāra doctrine.[18]

Ju Mipham uses the terms Cittamātra and Yogācāra interchangeably, indicating an understanding of its doctrine that would go beyond the standard descriptions found in the doxographies. This is in line with teachings from the oral tradition that distinguish between the Cittamātra of the tenet system (*grub mtha'i sems tsam*), which is to be refuted, and the Cittamātra of authoritative scriptures (*bka'i sems tsam*) such as the profound sutras of the third turning, which do not assert the existence of mind on the ultimate level.[19]

It is important to remember that the term *zhentong* is not used only in self-reference and that some masters seem to adopt conflicting positions in their writings. For instance, Mipham's stance on zhentong is not established conclusively, either in his own works or in modern academia. While he never declares himself a proponent of this view and even refutes it in several of his Madhyamaka writings, in other of his works he defends the zhentong position.[20]

We can say in conclusion that Yogācāra did survive in Tibet, not as a separate school but very much integrated into the views and systems of some of the greatest masters.[21]

MAITREYA'S *MADHYĀNTAVIBHĀGA*

The Text

The *Madhyāntavibhāga* is one in a set of five texts attributed, according to the Tibetan tradition, to Maitreya,[22] the future Buddha residing in Tuṣita heaven. These five are: *Ornament of Clear Realization* (*Abhisamayālaṃkāra; Mngon rtogs rgyan*), *Ornament of the Mahayana Sūtras* (*Mahāyānasūtrālaṃkāra; Mdo sde rgyan*), *Treatise on the Sublime Continuum of the Mahayana* (*Mahāyānottaratantraśāstra; Rgyud bla ma*), *Distinguishing the Middle from the Extremes* (*Madhyāntavibhāga; Dbus mtha' rnam 'byed*), and *Distinguishing Dharmas from Their True Nature* (*Dharmadharmatāvibhāga; Chos dang chos nyid rnam 'byed*).

Of these five, three are directly related to Yogācāra thought: the *Ornament of the Mahayana Sūtras, Distinguishing the Middle from the Extremes,* and *Distinguishing Dharmas from Their True Nature*. The principal theme of the *Treatise on the Sublime Continuum of the Mahayana* is *tathāgatagarbha,* or buddha-nature, and the *Ornament of Clear Realization* mainly relates to the Prajñāpāramitā literature (Perfection of Wisdom), another branch of Buddhist thought.

The Yogācāra tradition in general is renowned for having systematized all aspects of Buddhist thought and practice prevalent around the fourth century C.E. into a comprehensive system. The most famous example for this is Asaṅga's encyclopedic *Treatise on the Levels of Yoga Practice* (*Yogācārabhūmiśāstra*). The *Madhyāntavibhāga* also brings together an immense wealth of information covering virtually all aspects of the Mahayana, but in just a few pages. Its text is of middle length, composed of five chapters containing an average of twenty-two stanzas each.

As is so often the case with important Indian philosophical works written in verse (the so-called "root texts"), this text is very difficult if not impossible to understand without the help of a commentary. This closely reflects the method and spirit of learning in ancient India and Tibet. Root texts were not supposed to be the main source of information; the teacher was. These root texts, traditionally memorized by both the teacher and the student, served as a common basis for exposition, supplemented with the knowledge obtained through the study of oral and written commentaries. In the case of the *Madhyāntavibhāga*, we only know of two Sanskrit commentaries: one by Vasubandhu (fourth century) and the other by Sthiramati (sixth century), both included in the Tibetan canon.[23]

Authorship

Maitreya, the author of the *Madhyāntavibhāga*, is traditionally regarded as a bodhisattva of the highest order, who resides in Tuṣita, a divine realm beyond the reach of ordinary humans. The Indian master Asaṅga is said to have received his teachings from Maitreya there, to then bring them back to the world. This is the traditional account.

Modern academia paints a different picture. Scholars have put forth various explanations regarding Maitreya's identity. Some see him as Asaṅga's human teacher, others as a divine source for the latter's inspiration, and others still completely deny his existence, making Asaṅga the sole author of the works. At least, as Mathes points out, it is important to note that the works attributed to Maitreya differ in both form and content from Asaṅga's writings to a degree that one can hardly attribute them entirely to a single author.[24]

Overview of the Madhyāntavibhāga

The *Madhyāntavibhāga* has five chapters: Characteristics, Veils, Reality, Cultivation of the Antidotes, and the Unsurpassed Vehicle.

The first chapter discusses the characteristics of total affliction (*saṃkleśa; kun nas nyon mongs pa*) and complete purification (*vyavadāna; rnam par byang ba*), in other words the processes active in the perpetual cycle of suffering and dissatisfaction (samsara) and in the process of liberation from this state (nirvana). In this context, we are introduced to the concept of the imagination of the unreal (*abhūta-parikalpa; yang dag pa min pa'i kun tu rtog pa*), which is the fundamental mistake of conceptually constructing a dualistic reality in which the experienced and the experiencer, or the apprehended and apprehender, are two separate entities. While the existence of mind and experience is not questioned, the cognitive content of this conceptual process is refuted. It is here that we find a clear definition of emptiness in the unique Yogācāra fashion as the existence of the nonexistence of apprehended and apprehender (v.1.13). Emptiness is not a mere nonaffirming negation (*med dgag*), as it is explained in the Madhyamaka school.[25] It is the nonexistence of *something* (the imputed) in *something else* (the dependent), thereby affirming the existence of this "*something else,*" which is the imagination of the unreal. The most important concepts of the Yogācāra tradition are laid out in this first chapter, including the idea of mind-only, the three natures, and the eight-consciousness model.

The second chapter deals with the veils obstructing liberation and perfect enlightenment. Here, we learn about many different kinds of veils, all of which can be subsumed into two types: the veil of afflictions (*kleśāvaraṇa; nyon mongs pa'i sgrib pa*) and the cognitive veil (*jñeyāvaraṇa; shes bya'i sgrib pa*). The first type of veil consists of the mental factors such as desire, anger, and mistaken views of reality, all of which prevent one from gaining liberating direct insight into reality. The cognitive veil consists of the traces left on the mind by these afflictions. By removing these traces through the cultivation of the path, the obstructions to omniscience are gradually removed, eventually resulting in perfect awakening, or buddhahood. Those on the paths of the vehicles of the śrāvakas and pratyekabuddhas are mainly concerned with removing the first type of veil, while those on the bodhisattva path need to eliminate both. The following veils are explained in detail: five general veils, nine fettering obstructions that bring about suffering, thirty veils obstructing qualities, and veils peculiar to the factors conducive to awakening, the pāramitās, and the grounds (*bhūmi; sa*).

The third chapter is a thorough explanation of reality in terms of the three natures introduced in the first section of the *Madhyāntavibhāga*. The author begins with a brief presentation of the three natures themselves ("fundamental reality"), followed by an explanation of how an understanding of their characteristics removes distorted views of reality, subsumed in the extremes of denial and exaggeration ("reality in terms of its characteristics"). This section is followed by a presentation of the three natures in terms of the four aspects of the truth of suffering ("unmistaken reality," i.e., impermanence, suffering, emptiness, and selflessness), of the four ārya truths ("reality in terms of cause and result"), and of the two realities, ("coarse and subtle reality," i.e., conventional and ultimate reality). Then we are taught how reality is understood in different ways based on the means used to acquire knowledge ("reality as it is generally known"), and how it is correctly known by means of gnosis, the pristine wisdom attained through removal of the veils ("reality in terms of the domain of purity").

The next section briefly teaches how all objects of knowledge, subsumed into the five categories of knowledge peculiar to Yogācāra, are contained in the three natures ("reality in terms of containing reality"). After that, the three natures are taught in terms of the seven differentiated characteristics of reality taught in the *Saṃdhinirmocanasūtra* ("reality in terms of its differentiated characteristics"), followed by a longer explanation of the natures in terms of ten mistaken views based on the belief in a self and their appropriate antidotes ("reality in terms of expertise").

The fourth chapter presents the antidotes to be cultivated on the path, the stages of their application, and the results obtained in this process. The antidotes cultivated on the first four of the five paths to awakening (see glossary) are the thirty-seven factors conducive to awakening: the four close applications of mindfulness, the four perfect abandonments, and the four causes of miraculous power (cultivated on the path of accumulation); the five faculties and the five powers (cultivated on the path of joining); the seven limbs of awakening (accomplished on the path of seeing); and the eightfold ārya path (actualized on the path of cultivation). After this, the author explains eighteen stages of attainment, describing the path from beginning to end from various perspectives. The last section of this chapter gives an explanation of the results of practice. Here, the attainments are first explained in terms of the five types of result mentioned in the Abhidharma literature. Then the list is expanded to include ten further types of result.

The fifth chapter of the *Madhyāntavibhāga* elucidates the Mahayana, called the unsurpassed vehicle. It begins with an explanation of its superiority over the other vehicles in terms of practice, which fundamentally consists of the ten pāramitās ("perfections"). In this text, the pāramitās are taught in terms of twelve aspects that make them a supreme form of practice, followed by an explanation of their functions. After that, the mental engagement taught in the Mahayana is discussed in terms of the three wisdoms that arise from hearing, contemplation, and meditation. These wisdoms are accomplished by means of ten Dharma activities based on the Mahayana scriptures. The text then discusses the "factors concordant with reality," the practices of calm abiding ("being undistracted") and special insight ("being unmistaken"), the two branches of the meditative training on the path. Calm abiding is explained by means of the six distractions that are to be avoided, and special insight by means of ten divisions of unmistaken knowing. This is followed by an explanation of the Mahayana as a path free of all forms of dual extremes, and a brief note on the way the pāramitās relate to the bodhisattva grounds. After this long section on the unsurpassed practice, the superiority of the Mahayana is explained in terms of the unsurpassed supports and focal objects used on the path, and its unsurpassed accomplishments.

The text concludes with an explanation of the greatness of and necessity for this treatise.

RONGTÖN'S COMMENTARY

A Short Glimpse at the Life of Rongtön Sheja Künrig[26]

Traditionally, the career of a Buddhist scholar should encompass the three domains of exposition, debate, and composition called "the three activities of the learned." Inspired by this format, our account of Rongtön's life will start with these three categories, supplemented by a short section about his activities as the founder of a monastic institution, and another section on Rongtön "the saint," describing how he is perceived within his own tradition.

Rongtön, the Student and Teacher

Born in 1367 in Gyalmo Rong, in eastern Tibet, into a Bönpo family, Rongtön's religious path commenced at a young age, according to his biographer Shakya Chokden, by studying the Bönpo teachings. At the age of seventeen he traveled to one of the greatest centers of Buddhist learning in central Tibet, the seminary of Sangphu Ne'uthog. It was there he received monastic ordination and started his very thorough scholastic training, which would lead to his studying under more than twenty teachers.[27]

He proved to be such a bright student that he was able to compose his first major commentary, a subcommentary on the *Pramāṇaviniścaya* by Dharmakīrti, at the age of twenty-one. Yet it was not until the age of twenty-six that Rongtön met the most prominent of his teachers, the Sakya scholar Yaktön Sangye Pel (1348–1414). Under him Rongtön extensively studied the Prajñāpāramitā scriptures along with many commentaries, as well as several treatises on logic and epistemology (*pramāṇa; tshad ma*) and eventually became his successor.

Among all the subjects he was trained in (like all great Tibetan Buddhist scholars, he trained in both sutra and tantra), he was particularly renowned for his mastery of and commentaries on the Prajñāpāramitā philosophy of the *Abhisamayālaṃkāra*.

During his professional career, which lasted about sixty years, Rongtön's two main seats in central Tibet were the Sangphu seminary and the monastery of Nālendra (which he founded in 1436). In addition to his occasional travels to other seminaries and monasteries in the region, he made three visits to Tsang, which greatly contributed to his increasing fame. These visits consisted mainly of teaching and debating tours, and earned him the title "Rongtön Mawe Senge, the Teacher from [Gyalmo] Rong, Lion among Expounders," in addition to other titles.

Rongtön was able to confirm his academic status as a *kachupa* (*bka' bcu pa*: "master of ten scriptures") on these tours,[28] a challenge that had become a common practice to test the qualifications of advanced scholars in central Tibet at that time. The ten scriptures in question, which the bearer of this title was supposed to have mastered, covered all major fields of monastic study, namely Prajñāpāramitā philosophy (based on Maitreya's *Abhisamayālaṃkāra*), logic and epistemology (Pramāṇa), Abhidharma, Vinaya, Cittamātra and Tathāgatagarbha theory (based on the remaining four works attributed to Maitreya), as well as Madhyamaka.[29]

Assuming that Rongtön personally taught all the major treatises on which he composed commentaries, we can estimate that during his long teaching career he taught approximately sixty different classes to a vast number of disciples.[30] According to Shakya Chokden, he "had more students *who understood philosophical texts* than any Tibetan teacher of all time."[31] Many of the next generations' great scholars of all traditions (including Bön[32]), were either direct or indirect disciples of Rongtön, making him one of the most influential scholars of his time. These disciples include such illustrious names as Müchen Sempa Chenpo Könchog Gyaltsen (1388–1469); Gö Lotsawa Zhönu Pel (1392–1481); Shakya Chokden (1428–1507); and Gorampa Sönam Senge (1429–1489), who studied under Rongtön only very briefly. There were also many abbots from a number of great monasteries and seminaries, such as Sangphu, Ngor, Sera, Drepung, and others.[33] Even the name of the mahāsiddha Thangtong Gyalpo (1361–1485) appears in the list provided by Shakya Chokden among "those who gained faith in the master, having made a connection with him."

According to Jackson, almost all dialectic and scholastic lineages in the Sakya tradition pass through Rongtön, as well as the majority of these lineages in the Kagyü and Nyingma traditions.[34]

Rongtön, the Debater

In his own tradition, Rongtön is remembered as an undefeated debater.[35] By his rivals, however, he was probably remembered mainly for being the first scholar of major influence to directly oppose the ideas of Tsongkhapa Lobsang Dragpa (1357–1419), who would become one of the most important figures in the religious history of Tibet.[36] In fact, Shakya Chokden even mentions an account in which the two scholars allegedly met and debated in Lhasa, with Rongtön emerging from this debate as a winner—an account, however, not recorded in Tsongkhapa's biography. Whether or not this debate took place, there were other sources of controversy between Rongtön and members of the Ganden tradition, particularly Khedrup Je Geleg Palsang (1385–1438). These are laid out in more detail by Jackson.[37] For our purposes, it suffices to say that events with unfortunate outcomes led to great sectarian disputes between these two schools after Tsongkhapa's passing.

Rongtön, the Writer

Jackson gives us two lists of Rongtön's writings: one by Shakya Chokden included in his biography of the master, and another more recent one, compiled by Khenpo Appey Yonten Sangpo and others. Depending on the source, Rongtön is said to have authored either forty-one or forty-three major subcommentaries and nineteen minor treatises, as well as many smaller works, such as praises, *sādhanas*, personal communications, and so forth. All in all, Rongtön authored about three hundred works, which are said to have filled either thirteen or twenty volumes.[38]

Among his most important compositions are his commentaries on the *Abhisamayālaṃkāra* and those on the treatises attributed to Maitreya (one of which is the focus of the present work). Unfortunately, only about half of his oeuvre is available to us today, and of these, as Jackson notes, many are still difficult to access.

Rongtön, the Founder

One of Rongtön's most significant achievements was his founding of the monastic institution of Nālendra in Phenyul (Central Tibet) in 1436.

Jackson points out[39] that this was assisted by the loss of power of his former patrons, the Phamo Drupa.[40] Until 1434, Rongtön lived and taught either near Nedong, their main seat, or near Lhasa. When, due to an internal power struggle, the Phamo Drupa clan started to collapse and political conditions became unstable, Rongtön was invited to take up an alternative residence in the Phenyul Valley, to the north of the capital. In 1435 he was offered a piece of land there by a local lord, and soon the construction work on Nālendra began. Due to his fame and excellent reputation, Rongtön's efforts were greatly supported by the local nobility, as well as by monastic communities in the area.

After serving as an abbot for about eight years, Rongtön appointed his disciple Dagpo Penchen Tashi Namgyal (1399–1458) his successor in 1442, though he continued teaching at Nālendra until just a few days prior to his passing.

In a short account of Nālendra, the late Chogye Trichen Khyenrab Lekshe Gyatso (1919–2007)[41] states that from the time during which Rongtön served to the time of the seventh abbot, between two and three thousand monks were usually in residence there.[42] This number later varied, depending on the political stability of the region. In 1959, just prior to the Chinese communist takeover, seven hundred monks are believed to have resided at Nālendra.[43]

Rongtön, the Mystic and Saint[44]

Traditionally, Rongtön is regarded as an emanation of the future buddha, Maitreya, who resides in Tuṣita heaven. He is believed to have declared several times that his next incarnation will not take place in the human realm, and that he would rather be reborn as a god in the realm of Tuṣita. Rongtön is also believed to be the reincarnation of several panditas from India, including Kamalaśīla and Haribhādra, with whom he has common academic interests.[45]

With regard to his spiritual practice, Gö Lotsawa mentions that he exerted himself in the path of pacification (*zhi byed*),[46] having received the instructions from his principal teacher, Yaktön. From his intensive practice, which he was able to maintain while appearing to engage continuously in the activity of teaching, several signs of realization are said to have occurred. For instance, he was able to see the individual colors of the five wind energies (*rlung lnga*), and it is recorded that his fallen-off toenail transformed itself into a relic-like item. He was also able to foretell precisely the age at which he would pass away, namely eighty-three. All of these are considered to be great signs of spiritual accomplishment, indicating that Rongtön had reached the sixth level (*bhūmi*) of realization.

One can confidently say that Rongtön Sheja Künrig was one of the most outstanding Tibetan scholars of his time. He became known as the last of the "six ornaments of Tibet."[47] This refers to the six most illustrious teachers of the Sakya tradition, after its five founding masters.[48]

Rongtön's Commentary on the Madhyāntavibhāga

Regarded as an emanation of Maitreya, Rongtön is one of the few teachers in Tibet to have commented on each of the five treatises of Maitreya. In the tradition, his writings in general are considered to be highly authoritative, and those on the works of Maitreya particularly so. According to our sources, there are only four Tibetan commentaries on the *Madhyāntavibhāga*. Of those four, only the one by the early Sakya master Pang Lotsāwa Lodrö Tenpa (1276–1342) predates Rongtön's. Rongtön's has the advantage of being more concise and clearer than Pang Lotsāwa's, avoiding long and difficult points of debate. The two later commentaries on the *Madhyāntavibhāga* are fairly recent. One is by Ju Mipham (1846–1912), one of the most prolific authors of the Nyingma school, who revived the approach uniting the views of Yogācāra and Madhyamaka. He often follows Rongtön in his exposition of this text. The other is a brief "annotation commentary" by Khenpo Shenga (1871–1927), a widely respected master from the Nyingma tradition, famous for having penned commentaries for "the thirteen great Indian treatises" (*gzhung chen bcu gsum*).[49] The scarcity of commentaries is attributed to the fact that of the two main Mahayana schools, Yogācāra received less attention than the Madhyamaka school, for historical reasons.[50]

Rongtön is famous for commenting on the treatises of the various schools from their own perspective, not in order to establish a hierarchical system. While teaching this text, he assumes the role of a Yogācāra teacher, commenting on it according to its own tradition. His commentary is therefore of great interest to those eager to understand this tradition in a more unbiased manner.

ON THIS TRANSLATION

The Root Text

Traditionally, root texts are meant to be memorized when studying them by means of their commentaries. This is the reason why root texts are usually written in verse, which is easier to memorize than prose. Since students in Tibetan monastic universities were expected to know these texts by heart, their commentaries did not include the root verses. What was expected from a Tibetan monastic, however, cannot be assumed for a modern non-Tibetan reader, therefore we included a new translation of the root text to be used as a study support, inserted in the translation of the commentary.

We did not, however, compare the Tibetan text with the Sanskrit for this purpose, nor did we base our translation on a critical edition of the Tibetan stanzas. We did, of course, consult alternative editions of the root text (Peking: Q 5522, Narthang: N 4290) when the main edition (Derge: D 4021) seemed to contain obvious faults and readings at odds with Rongtön's commentary. In most cases, these corrections were silently integrated into our reading, without making notes for the reader. Since the translation of Rongtön's text was our main objective, we read the stanzas in light of his commentary without engaging in a critical study of the verses. The numbering of the stanzas follows Nagao's edition of the Sanskrit text.[51]

As stated earlier, root texts of this kind are usually very difficult, sometimes impossible, to understand by themselves. On top of that, the Tibetan translators of these verses would often omit grammatical particles to conform to the metric rules of composition, thus producing very cryptic poetry. This renders texts that are already difficult even more obscure. The importance of commentaries for the understanding and translation of these texts cannot be overstated. At the same time it is very important to keep in mind that every commentary represents a specific reading of the root verses. It is an interpretation.

The Commentary

We had access to three editions of the commentary for our translation. Initially we used the new edition of Rongtön's collected writings in ten volumes, published in Chengdu (Khren tu'u) in 2008. However, since this edition contains many faults, we quickly resorted to the reproduction of the nineteenth-century Derge blockprints, published by Dhongthog Rinpoche in New Delhi in 1979. This text contains few faults and is available through the Tibetan Buddhist Resource Center (TBRC), founded by the late Gene Smith (TBRC W24770).[52] During the final review phase of translation we also had access to a third edition, published in Chengdu in 1998.[53] This edition is in Western book format and contains chapter headings, which are very convenient for the study of the text. The spelling in this edition is better than that of the first editions mentioned here, but still inferior to Derge.

A Note on Notes, Brackets, and Diacritics

The endnotes in our translation contain information we hope readers will find useful in their studies. Many of these notes are based on private communications with Khenpo Jamyang Kunga, from whom the translator received explanations on the commentary. It is important for the reader to remember that this information stems from an oral tradition. There are often no written documents to verify the content of these notes. We therefore advise all students to validate their significance by means of further personal studies.

In an attempt to make this translation more reader friendly, we avoided as much as possible the use of square brackets, often used to add content in a translation wherever it is not explicit in the original. When we felt that content was implied in the Tibetan, in most cases we simply added it to the translation without further notice; however, there are a few cases where the additions are shown in square brackets.

Diacritics were used only with Sanskrit terminology that has not yet been included in mainstream English dictionaries, such as Oxford and Merriam-Webster. Terms such as samsara, nirvana, Mahayana, or samadhi, for example, can be found in these works and are therefore rendered without diacritics.

The Style of the Translation

As stated in the root text itself and confirmed in Rongtön's commentary, this material is difficult to understand. Texts of this nature are usually full of technical terms, expressions, and phrasings. It does not read like a novel and it is not supposed to. Certain passages will probably require repeated reading. But the same holds true for the Tibetan text itself. The average Tibetan layperson not educated in advanced Buddhist philosophy would have a very hard time understanding the content of these lines. Monastics often dedicate a decade or two to studying and understanding such philosophies. The study itself of such material, repeated reading and reflecting on the meaning of the words, is part of the process to sharpen one's intellectual faculties. If our heads are spinning as we study Yogācāra philosophy, good! It means that our mind is struggling as it tries to integrate new concepts that might be at odds with our innate or culturally acquired understanding of the world.

We did not try to make the material more difficult than it is by using unnecessarily abstruse language. We tried to use idiomatic English, while staying as close and as true to the text and its author as possible. The reader will see that we adopted an academic style, including technical phrases from the Tibetan debate context, which are completely unidiomatic in the English context, in order to convey the flavor of this text to readers.[54]

On Appendix 1: Illuminating the Essence

In addition to his detailed commentaries on virtually all aspects of Buddhist philosophy, Rongtön also authored a number of concise manuals distilling the essence of these texts relevant for the practice of meditation. Some of these manuals are directly based on the classical Indian treatises, outlining the stages of cultivation related to the topics taught in these texts. We found it to be beneficial to include Rongtön's brief *Illuminating the Essence* in the present volume, as it teaches precisely the stages of meditation based on the *Madhyāntavibhāga*. The Tibetan title of this text is *dbus dang mtha' rnam par 'byed pa'i sgom rim snying po rab tu gsal ba*. It is found in the section *sgrom khrid man ngag gi skor* in the first volume of Rongtön's collected works published in Chengdu (Khren tu'u) in 2008, and is also available on the TBRC website (W1PD83960). The entire collection of his meditation manuals and pith instructions is the subject of the translator's upcoming project for the Chödung Karmo Translation Group.

TRANSLATION

1

Opening Verses of Worship and Explanation of the Narrative

Oṃ svāsti!

With the moonlight of your exquisite form perfectly emerged from
  churning the ocean of milk of the two accumulations,
O friend, you bring to blossom my intelligence like a stainless kumuda
  flower.[1]
Mind Treasury, white as a snow mountain,
respectfully I present my offerings to you.[2]

The moon rays of your knowledge are like the ocean at play,
  agitated by the rolling dance of the garland of waves—your enlightened
  deeds.
The tree of your immeasurable compassion being fully grown,
  may you, Munīndra, Lord of Sages, ocean of wisdom and compassion, be
  victorious!

Towering lord of mountains of immeasurable love,
ablaze with the sun and moon rays of the two accumulations,
supreme in the center of the four continents of disciples,
may Ajita,[3] the chief among the Conqueror's heirs, be victorious!

Beautified by cloud garlands of vast erudition,
wondrous confidence flashing up like garlands of lightning,
continuously showering the timely rain of your eloquent exposition,
may the glorious guru, Lord of Clouds, be victorious!

Born, unprecedented, on the shore of the ocean of wisdom,
an adornment beautifying the ocean of discourses,

with a hundred petals of the eloquent exposition of Maitreya's excellent
   speech,
the sunlight of this explanation will distinguish the middle from the
   extremes.

When the Bhagavān Ajita (Maitreya) was known in a previous life as Bhikṣu
Sthiramati,[4] he focused his practice on the cultivation of the samadhi of
loving-kindness. Due to this, even those in his surroundings came to naturally abide in the state of this meditative absorption. It is for this reason that
he became renowned as Maitreya, the Loving One.

   With the beings to be trained in mind, he authored the *Five Dharmas of
Maitreya* from among which *Distinguishing the Middle from the Extremes*
(*Madhyāntavibhāga*) is the treatise I will explain here.

2

EXPLANATION OF THE TITLE

In Sanskrit: *Madhyāntavibhāgakārikā*
In Tibetan: *dbus dang mtha' rnam par 'byed pa'i tshig le'ur byas pa*

2.1. Translation of the title

The Sanskrit *madhya* means "middle," and *anta* means "extreme." *Vibhāga* means "to distinguish."

2.2. Explanation of the title

The treatise carries this name because it teaches the middle way by the means of eliminating the two extremes of permanence and annihilation.

To the [noble] youth Mañjuśrī I pay homage.

This phrase is the verse of worship inserted by the translators.

3
Explanation of the Treatise

This explanation includes a presentation of the main body of the treatise and an extensive explanation of its branches.

3.1. Presentation of the main body of the treatise

> Characteristics, veils, reality,
> cultivation of antidotes,
> their stages, the attainment of the result,
> and the unsurpassed vehicle.

The particular characteristics of phenomena, the veils obstructing that which is wholesome, reality, which is the focal object for the antidotes, the sequence of cultivation of the antidotes, the stages of the antidotes' arising, and the result obtained from the cultivation of the antidotes—these are the dharmas common to all vehicles. The unsurpassed vehicle is the Mahayana. The sequence of these points is like this for the following reasons:

In order to gain expertise in the characteristics of total affliction and complete purification at the very outset, the characteristics are taught first. As complete purification, in turn, will not be obtained as long as the veils have not been eliminated, the veils are taught next. The veils, in turn, are removed by focusing on reality, so reality is taught next. In case one wonders which antidotes bring about the exhaustion of the veils, the antidotes are taught after that. In case one wonders what the stages of the antidotes' arising may be, the stages of their arising are taught. In case one wonders which results are obtained from the antidotes, the results to be obtained are taught. In case one wonders what the uncommon path to obtain buddhahood may be, the unsurpassed vehicle is taught.

This completes the teaching presenting the main body of the treatise.

3.2. Extensive explanation of the branches

3.2.1. Explanation of the first chapter: Characteristics

The first of the five chapters, dealing with the characteristics, contains two divisions: explanations of the characteristics of total affliction and of the characteristics of complete purification.

3.2.1.1. The characteristics of total affliction

This section contains the following eight topics concerning total affliction: its characteristics in terms of existence and nonexistence, its particular characteristics, its characteristics in terms of what it comprises, its characteristics in terms of a means, its characteristics in terms of its subdivisions, its characteristics in terms of its categories, its characteristics in terms of its function, and the characteristics of total affliction.

3.2.1.1.1. The characteristics in terms of existence and nonexistence

> Imagination of the unreal exists.
> The two do not exist in it.
> Emptiness exists herein (i.e., in the imagination of the unreal).
> In it (emptiness), too, there is that (imagination of the unreal).
> (1.1)

In order to counteract denial, imagination of the unreal (*abhūta-parikalpa; yang dag pa min pa'i kun tu rtog pa*) is affirmed to exist substantially.

Q: Doesn't this contradict the teachings that say that all phenomena are emptiness?

A: It does not, because this emptiness actually refers to the fact that all phenomena are empty of both apprehended and apprehender. In order to counteract exaggeration, it is affirmed that apprehended and apprehender do not exist substantially in the imagination of the unreal.

In order to counteract denial with regard to the emptiness of apprehended and apprehender, emptiness is said to exist in the imagination of the unreal as its true nature (*dharmatā; chos nyid*).

And in that emptiness, too, there is imagination in the manner of that which possesses this property (i.e., the nature of emptiness).

> Therefore everything is explained
> as being neither empty nor not empty,
> because of existence, nonexistence, and existence.
> This is the middle way. (1.2)

Therefore imagination is explained as follows:

Since it is substantially existent, it is not empty. Since, however, it is also not the case that it is *not* empty of both apprehended and apprehender, the sutras state that all phenomena are neither empty nor not empty.

That which is beyond the two extremes of existence and nonexistence, the subject,[1] is the middle way, because it is the gateway to the realization of that which is free from the extremes of permanence and annihilation.

Q: In what way is it beyond existence and nonexistence?

A: It is beyond existence and nonexistence because imagination exists substantially; because both apprehended and apprehender do not exist; and because the emptiness empty of apprehended and apprehender does exist.

This explains the meaning of statements such as the following from the *Heap of Jewels* (*Ratnakūṭa*):

> Kāśyapa, to say "it exists" is one extreme.
> To say "it does not exist" is the other extreme.[2]

This completes the teaching on the characteristics of total affliction in terms of both existence and nonexistence.

3.2.1.1.2. Particular characteristics

> Consciousness appears as objects,
> sentient beings, self, and cognitions.
> Its objects do not exist,
> and since they do not exist, it too does not exist. (1.3)

Q: How many types of imagination of the unreal are there?

A: There are four, and they are the various types of consciousness which appear as objects, as sentient beings, as the self, and as cognitions. These, in turn, arise from the seed aspect of the all-base.

Consciousness appears as objects in the form of various outer objects such as form and so on. It appears as sentient beings in the form of the faculties such as the eye faculty, for example. That which appears as objects and sentient beings is the all-base consciousness. That which appears as the self is the afflicted mind, and that which appears as cognitions are the six types of consciousness.

The objects of the six types of consciousness, i.e., the appearance of consciousness as objects such as form and so forth, the subject, cannot be proved to exist the way they appear. This is because even though they appear as objects, they do not truly exist as such.[3] The same also applies to the faculties and so forth, which appear as sentient beings.[4] Because outer apprehended objects do not exist, the consciousness that apprehends them does not exist either. This is because the apprehender depends on the apprehended.

> **Therefore the existence of this imagination of the unreal is**
> **established.**
> **Neither is it as it appears nor is it absolutely nonexistent.**
> **Its end is regarded as liberation. (1.4)**

Although the apprehended aspect does not exist,[5] the essential nature of the consciousness that appears as objects, as sentient beings, as the self, and as cognitions, the subject, is established as substantially existent, because it is this imagination of the unreal. Apprehended and apprehender appear as two but do not exist as such. The basis of the appearance—imagination, however, is not absolutely nonexistent, as it arises as confusion. The end of this confused consciousness is regarded as the attainment of liberation.

This completes the teaching on the particular characteristics of total affliction.

3.2.1.1.3. The characteristics of total affliction in terms of what it comprises

> **It is, also, the imputed, the dependent, and the perfected.**
> **These are taught on account of objects,**
> **imagination of the unreal, and the nonexistence of both appre-**
> **hended and apprehender. (1.5)**

Imagination is explained as comprising the three natures in the following way. Imagination, the subject, may be presented in terms of the imputed, the dependent, and the perfected, because it appears as the entities of apprehended and apprehender. It is imagination of the unreal because it is the entity (Tib. *bdag nyid*) that is in actuality devoid of both apprehended and apprehender. That being so, the three natures are used to teach imagination.

This completes the teachings on the characteristics of total affliction in terms of what it comprises.

3.2.1.1.4. The characteristics of total affliction in terms of a means

> In dependence upon a focal object,
> nonconceptualization is born.
> In dependence upon nonconceptualization,
> nonconceptualization is born. (1.6)

> Thus it is established that the conceptualizing mind is of the
> nature of nonconceptualization.
> That being so, conceptualization and
> nonconceptualization must be understood as equal. (1.7)

The characteristics of total affliction in terms of a means are used to teach the method to engage in the purification of imagination.

The focal object (or object of reference) itself that appears as form is consciousness merely appearing in the form of objects by the power of latencies. In dependence on this understanding there arises a realization that does not conceptualize external objects. This is so because one refrains from clinging to objects by realizing that appearances are merely the mind.

In dependence on understanding the objects of apprehension as nonconceivable, there arises a realization that does not conceptualize an apprehender either. This is because by not conceptualizing an apprehended object, one penetrates the fact that the apprehender too is non-conceivable. As there is no object to conceive, the conceiving mind is established as being of a non-conceivable nature. This is because there is no apprehender without an apprehended.

In the absence of an apprehended object, no conceiving of it will occur either. That being so, both the conceived object and that which conceives it must equally be understood as being of that very non-conceivable nature.

This completes the teachings on the characteristics of total affliction in terms of a means.

3.2.1.1.5. The characteristics of total affliction in terms of its subdivisions

> Imagination of the unreal is
> the mind and mental factors of the three realms. (1.8ab)

Imagination of the unreal has two aspects: mind and mental factors.

Q: Are the mind and mental factors without taints[6] also included?

A: No, they are not, as only the three realms possess the characteristic of separating apprehended and apprehender.

This completes the teachings on the characteristics of total affliction in terms of its subdivisions.

3.2.1.1.6. The characteristics of total affliction in terms of its categories

> There, consciousness perceives the object,
> and mental factors its particular features. (1.8cd)

The categories are taught in order that we understand that mind and mental factors are the categories of imagination.

Q: What are mind and mental factors?

A: Of these two, consciousness merely perceives an object,[7] and the mental factors are the perceiving entities that possess specific modes of apprehension that perceive its particular features.

Focusing on a form, mind arises as having the aspect of that form. Since, however, it does not have distinct features for particular modes of apprehension, it is explained as merely perceiving the object.[8] Mental factors do possess specific individual modes of apprehension for the particular features, which the mind does not have. This is why the text says "its particular features."

Q: What are the particular features of the modes of apprehension?

A: They are, for example, the way the mental factor of discrimination apprehends signs, or the way sensation experiences an object.

However, this does not mean that having distinguished two objects—general and particular—there are two distinct apprehensions of the general and the particular that are asserted to be the distinctive features of mind and mental factors.[9] The extensive refutation and establishment of this point is laid out in the *Ornament to the Seven Treatises* (*sde bdun gyi rgyan*).[10]

This completes the teaching on the characteristics of total affliction in terms of its categories.

3.2.1.1.7. The characteristics of total affliction in terms of its function

One [type of consciousness] is consciousness as a causal condition,
the second is the experiencer.
Experiencing, determining,
and [the other factors that] cause its engagement are the mental
    factors. (1.9)

The characteristics of total affliction in terms of its function explain the way in which the imagination of the unreal functions in terms of cause and result. This function, in turn, has two aspects: the function as a continuum of moments and its function over the course of various lives. We will discuss this topic based on the first of these.[11]

One type of consciousness is the all-base consciousness, the subject. It is called *consciousness as causal condition* because it is the cause for the other seven consciousnesses. The second, the group of these seven consciousnesses, the subject, is called *experiencer of objects*. This is because they engage with their objects, such as form and so on, in a clear way.

Sensation is called *experiencing*, because it is that which has the essential nature of experiencing the maturation of deeds. Discrimination is called *determining*, because it determines an object by apprehending signs. The other mental factors such as volition or attention, the subject, cause the essential nature of that consciousness to engage with the object, because they manifestly apply the mind to an object.

This completes the teaching on the characteristics of total affliction in terms of its function.

3.2.1.1.8. The characteristics of total affliction

Because of veiling, planting,
leading, and seizing,
because of completing, determining based on three,
experience, and consolidation,
because of binding, directing,
and suffering, beings are afflicted. (1.10–1.11b)

The characteristics of total affliction are taught in order that we may know what causes total affliction. We will examine the twelve links of dependent arising here.

1. Ignorance (*avidyā; ma rig pa*) is said to afflict beings because it veils their vision of reality.

2. Formative factors (*saṃskāra; 'du byed*) afflict beings because they plant the seeds for rebirth in the consciousness, consciousness here referring to the all-base.

3. The all-base consciousness (*vijñāna; rnam shes*), repository of karmic latencies, the subject, afflicts beings because it leads them to a place of rebirth.

4. Name and form (*nāma-rūpa; ming gzugs*) afflict beings because they seize the body of the next existence.

5. The six sense sources (*āyatana; skye mched*) afflict beings because they bring the condition of name and form to completion.

6. Contact (*sparśa; reg pa*), the subject, afflicts beings because it determines the object based on the coming together of object, sense faculty, and consciousness.

7. Sensation (*vedanā; tshor ba*) afflicts beings because it experiences the pleasant and unpleasant maturation of deeds.

8. Craving (*tṛṣṇā; sred pa*) afflicts beings because it consolidates birth in a new existence by nurturing the seeds thereof.

9. Clinging (*upādāna; nye bar len pa*) afflicts beings because it binds them to the new existence.

10. Becoming[12] (*bhava; srid pa*) afflicts beings because it actualizes a new existence in the next birth without being interrupted by another birth.

11. Birth (*jāti; skye ba*), the subject, afflicts beings because it binds them to the suffering of aging and death, and so forth.

12. Aging and death (*jarā-maraṇa; rga shi*), the subject, afflict beings because they are the actualization of the maturation of deeds.

> **The three, two, and seven aspects of affliction
> all come from imagination of the unreal.** (1.11cd)

The twelve links comprise the afflictions of total affliction, the total affliction of karma, and the total affliction of birth in the following way. Ignorance, craving, and clinging comprise the total affliction of total affliction.

Formative factors and becoming are also total affliction because they are the total affliction of karma. The seven remaining links, that is, consciousness and so on, the subject, are total affliction because they are the total affliction of (birth or) life.[13]

Alternatively, it is explained that not only ignorance, craving, and clinging are causal total affliction, but formative factors and becoming are as well. The other seven links, that is, consciousness and so on, are resultant total affliction.

The root of all three aspects of affliction is imagination, because they arise from imagination of the unreal.

This completes the teaching on the characteristics of total affliction.

3.2.1.2. The characteristics of complete purification

3.2.1.2.1. Brief summary

Briefly, emptiness should be understood by its characteristics,
its synonyms and their meaning, its divisions, and the proofs.
(1.12)

How is one to understand emptiness free of total affliction? Briefly, emptiness must be understood by means of five explanations, which present it in terms of its characteristics, its synonyms, the meaning of its synonyms, its divisions, and in terms of lines of reasoning to prove it.

3.2.1.2.2. Detailed explanation

3.2.1.2.2.1. The characteristics of emptiness

The characteristics of emptiness are the nonexistence of the two
and the existence of [that] nonexistence.
Neither existent nor nonexistent,
it is not defined as being either different or identical. (1.13)

The existence (*dngos po*) of the nonexistence (*dngos med*) of apprehended and apprehender, the subject, is the characteristic of emptiness. Why? Because it is empty of both apprehended and apprehender, and because it is the essential nature devoid of the existence of apprehended and apprehender. What is termed *existence* in this context refers to the negation of clinging to emptiness as nonexistence, like to the horns of a rabbit.

Emptiness has four distinctive features:

1. It does not exist as the essential nature of both apprehended and apprehender, because it is empty of both apprehended and apprehender.

2. Nor is it nonexistent as the essential nature empty of these two, because if it were not empty of both, then apprehended and apprehender would exist, since negating the negation is tantamount to establishing existence.

3. Emptiness empty of apprehended and apprehender, the subject, does not possess the characteristic of being an entity distinct from imagination of the unreal, because it (i.e., that emptiness) is the very nature of both apprehended and apprehender.

4. It also does not possess the characteristic of being identical with imagination of the unreal, because even though imagination is established through experience by ordinary beings,[14] it (emptiness) is not established by them.[15]

3.2.1.2.2.2. The synonyms

> The synonyms of emptiness are, in brief,
> thusness, the highest limit of reality,
> the signless, the ultimate,
> and *dharmadhātu*. (1.14)

> Not other, not mistaken,
> the cessation [of signs], the āryas' domain,
> and the cause of the ārya dharmas.
> These are, respectively, the meanings of the synonyms. (1.15)

Emptiness is taught in brief by listing its synonyms, which are: thusness, the highest limit of reality, the signless, ultimate reality, and dharmadhātu. These are the synonyms, because they refer to the same thing with different terms.

Let us discuss the meaning of these terms one by one.

1. Emptiness empty of the apprehended and apprehender, the subject, is referred to as *thusness* (or "as-it-is-ness," *tathatā; de bzhin nyid*) because it is that which does not change from a previous state into something else.

2. It is referred to as *the highest limit of reality* (*bhūtakoṭi; yang dag pa'i mtha'*) because being the way things really are, it is not mistaken.

3. It is referred to as *the signless* (*animitta; mtshan ma med pa*) because it is by nature the cessation of the distinguishing signs of conceptual proliferation.

4. It is referred to as *the ultimate* (*paramārtha; don dam pa*) because it is the domain of an ārya's sublime gnosis.

5. It is referred to as *dharmadhātu* because it is the cause[16] of the *dharmas* (properties) of an ārya, and because the dharmas of an ārya arise when one takes it as one's focal object.

3.2.1.2.2.3. The divisions of emptiness

Emptiness will be explained by means of a twofold division, a fourteenfold division, and the two remaining divisions.

3.2.1.2.2.3.1. The twofold division of emptiness

Owing to total affliction and complete purification,
it is either stained or stainless.
Like the purity of water, gold, and the sky, it is considered to be
  pure. (1.16)

3.2.1.2.2.3.1.1. The actual division

Two types of emptiness are distinguished, stained and stainless, because it is distinguished in terms of either being associated with total affliction or as being purified of total affliction by means of the antidotes.

3.2.1.2.2.3.1.2. Dispelling objections

Q: If previously stained, how can it later become stainless?

A: Water may be muddy, gold may seem tarnished, and the sky may be covered in clouds. But as these stains are not their nature, they are posited as utterly pure. In the same way, because the nature of mind, too, is free of stains, the stains can be removed, and therefore it is by nature utterly pure. Thus, because the antidotes remove the stains, it is correct to assert that [mind] can later be purified of the stains.

3.2.1.2.2.3.2. Fourteen divisions of emptiness

> Emptiness of the consumer, of the consumed,
> of the body related to these, and of the abode.
> Moreover, that which sees reality as it is
> and that which is seen as well are emptiness. (1.17)

1. The six faculties, that is, the eye faculty and so on, the subject, are termed *consumer* because they experience their respective objects. Since the consumer is subsumed by the *inner* aspect of experience, its emptiness is termed *inner emptiness.*

2. The objects, such as form or sound, and so on, the subject, are termed *consumed* because they are the objects to be experienced by the faculties. Since the consumed is subsumed by the *outer,* its emptiness is termed *outer emptiness.*

3. The body, which is the support for both the consumer and the consumed, the subject, is termed *outer and inner* because it is not included in the faculties on the one hand, but is included in mind and its continuum on the other. Its emptiness is termed *emptiness of both outer and inner.*

4. The abode, which is the container world, the subject, is called *great* because it is vast. Its emptiness is termed the *emptiness of the great.*

5. The mind that sees outer and inner phenomena as emptiness, the subject, is called *emptiness* because it is the perceiver of emptiness. Here, the subject is labeled with the name of the object. Its emptiness is termed the *emptiness of emptiness.*

6. Emptiness seen as the ultimate, the subject, is termed *the ultimate.* Why? Because in order to see the ultimate, one focuses on emptiness, the domain of gnosis. This emptiness is referred to as *the ultimate,* therefore it is labeled with that name. Its emptiness is the *emptiness of the ultimate.*

> To obtain twofold wholesomeness, to constantly benefit beings,
> in order not to abandon samsara and not to exhaust goodness,
>   (1.18)
> to purify the spiritual disposition (*gotra; rigs*), to obtain the
>   major and minor marks,
> and to purify the qualities of a buddha:
> these are the objectives the bodhisattvas strive to accomplish.
>   (1.19)

Why do bodhisattvas need to rely on the meditation on emptiness in order to accomplish the path?

7. In order that we can meditate on the emptiness of the compounded, the *emptiness of the compounded* is taught.

8. In order that we can meditate on the emptiness of the uncompounded, the *emptiness of the uncompounded* is taught.

Q: Why are these two cultivated?

A: One cultivates them to obtain compounded and uncompounded wholesome qualities, and by meditating on both types of emptiness, one purifies the clinging to the compounded and the uncompounded, making them thus manifest as free of stains. In other words, in order to attain the purification of the stains of clinging to compounded and uncompounded wholesomeness, one meditates on the emptiness of the compounded and of the uncompounded. For this purpose these two types of emptiness are taught gradually. Compounded wholesome qualities are the path and uncompounded wholesomeness is nirvana.

9. That which is beyond the extremes of existence (samsara) and peace (nirvana) is beyond extremes. Its emptiness is the *emptiness of that which is beyond extremes*. This is to be meditated upon in order to constantly benefit beings.

10. Samsara is without beginning and end. Its emptiness is the *emptiness of that which is without beginning and end*. One meditates on it in order not to completely abandon samsara for the sake of beings. Were one not to realize samsara as emptiness, one would see it as riddled with faults and strive to be rid of it.

11. The roots of wholesomeness, which are inexhaustible even at the time of nirvana without remainder, are not discarded. Their emptiness is the *emptiness of that which is not discarded*. It is meditated upon in order to make them inexhaustible even when the state without remainder is achieved. This is because this meditation purifies the stains of apprehended and apprehender with regard to the roots of wholesomeness, and brings about the attainment of the dharmakāya, making the roots of wholesomeness uninterrupted.

12. The naturally present spiritual disposition is that which is *natural* and its emptiness is the *emptiness of the natural*. It is to be meditated upon in order to thoroughly purify even a buddha's spiritual disposition, as this meditation purifies the stains of clinging to the spiritual disposition.

13. The major and minor marks are the particular characteristics [of the result of complete purification], and its emptiness is the *emptiness of the*

particular characteristics. It is meditated upon in order to obtain completely pure major and minor marks, because this meditation completely purifies the clinging to the major and minor marks as truly existent.

14. The entire range of a buddha's qualities consists of the ten powers, four fearlessnesses, the eighteen unique qualities, and so on. The emptiness of these is the *emptiness of all qualities*. It is meditated upon in order to purify the qualities of a buddha, because this meditation purifies the clinging to these qualities, bringing about their complete purification.

Thus, bodhisattvas accomplish the path by taking these types of emptiness as their point of reference for the sake of obtaining the above-mentioned qualities such as compounded and uncompounded wholesomeness, and so forth.

3.2.1.2.2.3.3. The two remaining divisions of emptiness

> Here, emptiness is the nonexistence of the individual and
> phenomena.
> The existence of that nonexistence is yet another type of empti-
> ness. (1.20)

1. The nonexistence of the "self of the individual" and the "self of phenomena" is referred to as the *emptiness of that which is nonexistent*.

2. The existence of the nonexistence of the two selves is the *emptiness of the essential nature of nonexistence*. Therefore it is said to be different from the above-mentioned forms of emptiness. The first of these two is taught in order to dispel exaggeration with regard to the individual and phenomena, and the second in order to counteract denial regarding emptiness.

3.2.1.2.2.4. The proof to establish emptiness

> If there were no affliction, all embodied beings would be
> liberated.
> If there were no purification, effort would be fruitless. (1.21)

Q: If the mind is naturally pure, how is it that it is later totally afflicted and then purified?

A: If emptiness were initially not afflicted, then all embodied beings would be effortlessly liberated, because there would be no binding afflictions from the beginning.

Q: If the mind is initially afflicted, how can it later be purified?

A: If these afflictions were not purified at a later stage despite the cultivation of the antidotes, it would follow that it would be fruitless to exert effort on the path to remove them.

> Neither afflicted, nor unobscured.
> Neither pure, nor impure. (1.22ab)

Q: How can it be both naturally pure and afflicted?

A: The emptiness of the mind, the subject, is not afflicted in essence, because it is luminous. Therefore its nature is not impure. It is, however, not unafflicted, because it does possess adventitious afflictions. It is therefore also not stainless.

In other words, the nature of the mind, which is emptiness, the subject, is by nature not impure, because its essence, being luminous, is unafflicted. It is also not stainless, because it has adventitious afflictions, *adventitious* meaning that they can be removed.

> These are the stanzas on characteristics, the first chapter of
> *Distinguishing the Middle from the Extremes.*

This completes the commentary on the first chapter, the stanzas on characteristics.

3.2.2. Explanation of the second chapter: The veils

3.2.2.1. General presentation

> Pervasive, limited, excessive,
> equal, taking up and rejecting:
> these are explained to be the veils of the two [vehicles]. (2.1a–c)

The twofold veil[17] of those possessing the bodhisattva's spiritual disposition, the subject, is called the *pervasive veil* because it obstructs the accomplishment of benefit for oneself and others.

The veil of those possessing the śrāvaka spiritual disposition,[18] the subject, is called the *limited veil* because it obstructs the accomplishment of one's personal benefit only.

Excessive afflictions such as the attachment of the three types of beings possessing a spiritual disposition,[19] the subject, comprise the *excessive veil* because they are veils that arise to an excessive degree, even toward insignificant objects.

Afflictions of the three types of beings possessing a spiritual disposition that arise to a degree congruent with the object, the subject, are called the *equal veil,* because their intensity corresponds to the importance of the object.

The two *veils of taking up the cause of samsara* and *of intentionally rejecting samsara*, the subject, are the veils that obstruct the arising of the bodhisattva path, because they are in conflict with the bodhisattvas' wisdom and means. With their wisdom, bodhisattvas realize that samsara is devoid of self-nature, and out of compassion, the means, they do not abandon beings.

The first veil and the last two (*pervasive, taking up,* and *rejecting*) conflict with the bodhisattva path. The second (*limited*) conflicts with the paths of śrāvakas and pratyekabuddhas. The *excessive* and *equal veils* are explained to be common to both the greater and the smaller vehicles.

3.2.2.2. Individual explanation

3.2.2.2.1. The veil of afflictions

3.2.2.2.1.1. The obstructing fetters

> Nine types of fetters have the characteristics of affliction.
> These fetters are obstructions. (2.1d–2.2a)

Q: How many kinds of veils of afflictions are there?

A: The veils that have the characteristic of affliction must be identified as the nine types of fettering obstructions.

Q: What are these nine?

A: The nine types of fettering obstructions are (1–5) the five afflictions not associated with a view,[20] (6) views, (7) regarding as supreme, (8) jealousy, and (9) miserliness. These nine are referred to as fetters because they bind one to all kinds of sufferings. In this context, *views* refers to three different views,[21] and *regarding as superior* to holding discipline and ascetic practices as supreme.[22]

3.2.2.2.1.2. The obstructed qualities

Dissatisfaction, equanimity, and seeing reality,
the view of the perishing collection and its basis, (2.2b–d)
cessation, path, and the Precious Jewels;
honor and gain, and a thorough understanding of
the value of having fewer material possessions. (2.3a–c)

Q: What do the afflictions obstruct?

A: The fetter of *desire* obstructs the arising of dissatisfaction with samsara, because of the attachment to samsara it generates. *Anger* obstructs the mind from abiding in equanimity because it agitates the mind from within. The remaining seven all obstruct one from seeing reality.

With regard to their individual functions:

Pride obstructs one from understanding the faults of the view of the perishing collection, because it obstructs the understanding of the faults of self-grasping.

Ignorance obstructs the thorough understanding of the real nature of the five skandhas of clinging, the basis for the view of the perishing collection. This is because ignorance generates wrong views, such as clinging to permanence.[23]

The fetter of *views* obstructs the actualization of the truth of cessation, because the *view of the perishing collection* and *clinging to extreme views* leave one terrified at the idea of cessation and produce a fear of the annihilation of the self, as do *wrong views,*[24] because they deny cessation.

The two aspects of view of *superiority* obstruct the truth of the path, because they hold as superior certain practices that conflict with the path.

Doubt obstructs the understanding of the qualities of the Three Precious Jewels, because it makes one not believe in those qualities.

Jealousy obstructs the thorough understanding of the faults of honor and gain, because it generates attachment to one's personal honor and gain, and anger toward the excellence of others.

The fetter of *miserliness* obstructs the thorough understanding of the value of drastically reducing one's material possessions, because it generates excessive attachment to them.

Here, the two fetters of *attachment* and *hatred* hinder one from engaging in the preparation for the realization of reality, while the remaining ones obstruct one from gaining it.

This completes the explanation of the veil of afflictions.

3.2.2.2.2. The veils obstructing wholesome qualities and the others

3.2.2.2.2.1. Explanation of the thirty veils

> Other veils obstruct the ten qualities, beginning with whole-
> some qualities. (2.3d)

This means that the veils inhibiting the ten obstructed qualities, beginning with *wholesome qualities,* are explained as being different from the above-mentioned nine fetters. In other words, the veils obstructing the ten qualities, that is, the wholesome qualities and so on, are different from the veil of afflictions.

> [The veils are:]
> **Not applying, and that which is not the basis,**
> **whatever is produced by wrong practices,**
> **nonarising, lack of mental engagement,**
> **and incomplete accumulations; (2.4)**

(1a) *Not applying* refers to the veil consisting in not applying oneself to that which is wholesome out of heedlessness and laziness. [25]

(1b) *That which is not the basis* refers to the veil consisting of attachment to non-Buddhist teachings, which are not the means for obtaining awakening.

(1c) *Whatever is produced by practices that are not appropriate uses of mental engagement* refers to the veil consisting of applying oneself to that which is not a method for discarding the afflictions. [26]

(2a) The *nonarising* of the roots of wholesomeness also obstructs awakening, because without wholesome potential, awakening will not be obtained.

(2b) *Lack of mental engagement* also obstructs awakening, because laziness does not allow one to refine the roots of wholesomeness.

(2c) *Incomplete accumulations* refer to the veil consisting in not having fully accumulated the causes of the two accumulations.

> Not having the spiritual disposition, not having a teacher,
> feeling utterly disheartened,
> not having a practice,
> and associating with negative and aggressive people; (2.5)

(3a) *Not having the spiritual disposition* refers to the veil consisting of lacking the Mahayana spiritual disposition.

(3b) *Not having a teacher for the wholesome path* means that although one does possess the Mahayana spiritual disposition, one lacks a guide who will introduce one perfectly to the wholesome path of the Mahayana.

(3c) *Feeling utterly disheartened* means that despite having met with a teacher for the wholesome path, one feels utterly disheartened due to the hardships of the Mahayana, or alternatively, due to the hardships of exerting oneself in cultivating the roots of wholesomeness.

(4a) *Not having a practice* refers to the veil consisting of not engaging in the pāramitās.

(4b) *Associating with negative people* refers to the veil consisting of associating with those who do not understand the qualities of the bodhisattvas.

(4c) *Associating with aggressive people* refers to the veil consisting of associating with people who wrongly criticize bodhisattvas.

In this way, associating with negative and aggressive people is presented separately.

> One's three negativities,
> and what remains of these three,
> not bringing wisdom to maturation;
> natural negativities,
> laziness, and heedlessness; (2.6)

(5a) *One's three negativities* refers to the veils of afflictions, of karma, and of maturation.[27]

(5b) *What remains of these three* refers to whatever remains of the three veils.[28]

(5c) *Not bringing wisdom to complete maturation* refers to the veil consisting in not bringing the wisdoms of study and contemplation to complete maturation.

(6a) *Natural* or innate *negativities* refers to the veil consisting in the dormant latencies of afflictions, which must be discarded by means of the path of cultivation.

(6b) *Laziness* refers to the veil consisting in not delighting in that which is wholesome.

(6c) *Heedlessness* refers to the veil consisting in not protecting one's mind from defiling factors.[29]

> Attachment to existence and pleasure,
> faint-heartedness,
> lack of faith, lack of conviction,
> and following the literal meaning; (2.7)

(7a) *Attachment to existence* refers to the veil consisting of clinging to the five skandhas.

(7b) *Attachment to pleasure* refers to the veil consisting of clinging to the sense objects such as form and so on.

(7c) *Faint-heartedness* refers to the veil consisting of the inability to engage in vast wholesome activities.

(8a) *Lack of faith* refers to the veil consisting of a lack of trust and faith in the Mahayana methods.

(8b) *Lack of conviction* refers to the veil consisting of holding the profound and vast Excellent Speech of the Buddha to be mistaken.[30]

(8c) *Following the literal meaning* refers to the veil consisting of forming concepts based on the literal meaning of expressions like "the unborn" or "primordial peace," not understanding the intended meaning behind such terms.

> Not holding the sacred Dharma in high esteem,
> craving gain, and lacking compassion,
> lack of studies, little learning,
> and not being trained in samadhi. (2.8)

(9a) *Not holding the sacred Dharma in high esteem* refers to the veil consisting of not regarding the Dharma as being very valuable.

(9b) *Craving gain* refers to the veil consisting of making gain alone one's priority.

(9c) *Lacking compassion* refers to the veil consisting of having an impure motivation for teaching the Dharma.

(10a) *Lack of studies* refers to the veil consisting of not studying the sacred Dharma as a result of having accumulated the karma of rejecting the Dharma.

(10b) *Little learning* refers to the veil consisting of the inability to grasp the vast teachings, although one has studied a little bit.

(10c) *Not being completely trained in samadhi* refers to the veil consisting of not being trained in the four causes of miraculous power, that is, interest, diligent perseverance, and so forth.

This completes the explanation of the thirty veils.

3.2.2.2.2.2. The ten obstructed qualities, wholesome qualities, and the others

> Wholesome qualities and so on refers to the ten following qualities:
> wholesome qualities, awakening, perfectly embracing,
> being wise, absence of delusion, absence of veils,
> dedication, fearlessness, absence of miserliness, and mastery. (2.9)

1. *Wholesome qualities* refers to everything wholesome that functions as the cause of awakening.

2. *Awakening* is the comprehension of reality exactly as it is.

3. To *perfectly embrace awakening* means to generate the mind that is the cause of awakening.

4. *Being wise* refers to bodhisattvas, because of their sharp faculties.

5. *Absence of delusion* refers to the path of seeing, because seeing reality directly gives rise to a mind which is non-erroneous.

6. *Absence of veils* refers to the path of cultivation, because it acts as the antidote to all possible veils. Alternatively, it may be applied to the lack of remaining veils.[31]

7. *Dedication* refers to skill in means, because it turns the wholesome into the cause of accomplishing awakening.

8. *Fearlessness* means that one is not frightened by the Buddha's profound and vast discourses.

9. *Absence of miserliness* means that one teaches the sacred Dharma without being concerned with gain and honor.

10. *Mastery* refers to buddhahood, because it is the complete perfection of the ten powers.[32]

Thus the ten properties, from wholesome qualities up to mastery, are the ten obstructed qualities.

At this point, Ācārya Vasubandhu lays out ten productive causes[33] together with examples related to the ten obstructed qualities.[34]

1. An example of the productive cause of arising is the eye faculty, from which visual consciousness arises.

2. An example of the productive cause of maintaining existence is the four types of sustenance[35] that sustain the body (or existence).

3. An example of the productive cause of support is the ground of the container world, which supports the contained beings.

4. An example of the productive cause of illumination is a lamp, which illuminates the form that is to be shown.

5. An example of the productive cause of transformation is fire, which cooks and burns.

6. An example of the productive cause of separation is a sickle, used to cut grass.

7. An example of the productive cause of transformation is a goldsmith, who turns a lump of gold into various objects, such as bracelets.

8. An example of the productive cause of conviction is smoke serving as evidence by means of which the presence of fire can be inferred.

9. An example of the productive cause of understanding is the reasoning consisting of thesis and proof that brings about certainty.

10. An example of the productive cause of attainment is the path based on which one attains nirvana.

Thus we read:

> For the ten productive causes of arising,
> maintaining existence, support, that which is shown,
> transformation, separation, change,
> conviction, understanding, and attainment,
> the examples of eye, sustenance, ground, lamp,
> and fire, and so on, are given.
> The others are sickle, craft, smoke,
> reasoning, and path.[36]

[Vasubandhu] further teaches the sequence in which the ten obstructed qualities, such as the productive cause of the arising of the wholesome, the productive cause of maintaining the existence of the awakened state, and so on, and the ten veils obstructing arising, maintaining the existence, and so on, are connected.

This sequence is as follows:

Having first engaged oneself in cultivating the roots of wholesomeness, one proceeds to completely embrace the generation of bodhicitta, the mind resolved to attain supreme awakening, because it is the foundation for the perfect accomplishment of the two purposes (i.e., one's own and others' benefit). Then, in order to fulfill the promise of bodhicitta, one practices the activities of the bodhisattvas consisting of giving and so forth. After that, as the result of the two accumulations consisting of the practice of the pāramitās of giving and the others, the path of seeing free of confusion is generated. This is followed by training on the path of cultivation free from the remaining veils.[37]

Then, in order not to waste the roots of wholesomeness generated in those circumstances, one dedicates the wholesome qualities to awakening.[38] As this dedication depends on having studied the vast and profound discourses, one engages in their studies without fear. Having studied those discourses, one teaches the Dharma in order to bring sentient beings to maturity. Having brought to maturity those who are to be tamed by the Dharma, one attains buddhahood, which is the attainment of mastery.

This completes the explanation of the ten obstructed qualities, the wholesome qualities, and the others.

3.2.2.2.2.3. Explanation of which veils obstruct which quality

The veils pertaining to those ten qualities
Must be understood as being threefold each time. (2.10ab)

Q: Which veils obstruct the wholesome qualities, and which the other qualities?

A: It must be understood that there are three veils for each of the ten obstructed qualities, the wholesome qualities, and so on. That is to say:

1. The three veils obstructing the *wholesome qualities* are not applying, applying oneself to that which is not the basis of awakening, and the veil consisting of that which is produced by inappropriate practices.[39]

2. The three veils obstructing *awakening* are not generating the roots of wholesomeness, a lack of mental engagement even though they have been generated, and not completing the accumulations.

3. The three veils obstructing *perfectly embracing* are not possessing a spiritual disposition, not having a teacher for the wholesome path, and feeling utterly disheartened.

4, The three veils obstructing the bodhisattvas' *deeper understanding* are not having a practice, associating with negative people, and associating with aggressive people.

5. The three veils obstructing the *absence of delusion* are the three mistaken negativities, whatever remains of the three veils, and not bringing wisdom to maturation. One's own three negativities are the veils of afflictions, of karma, and of maturation.

6. The three veils obstructing the *absence of veils* are natural negativities, laziness, and heedlessness.

7. The three veils obstructing *dedication* are attachment to existence, attachment to pleasure, and faintheartedness.

8. The three veils obstructing *fearlessness* are having no faith in the individual,[40] having no conviction in the Dharma, and taking the teachings literally.

9. The three veils obstructing the *absence of miserliness* are not holding the Dharma in high esteem, craving honor and gain, and lacking compassion.

10. The three veils obstructing *mastery* are lacking studies, little learning, and not being trained in samadhi.

This completes the explanation of the veils obstructing the arising of wholesome qualities and so forth.

3.2.2.2.3. Veils on the path

3.2.2.2.3.1. General presentation

> **The veils obstructing the factors conducive to awakening,**
> **the pāramitās, and the grounds, are different ones. (2.10cd)**

The veils obstructing the factors conducive to awakening,[41] the pāramitās, and the grounds are different from the two types of veils mentioned above (i.e., the veil of afflictions and the thirty veils, beginning with the veils obstructing the arising of wholesome qualities, and so forth).

3.2.2.2.3.2. Detailed explanation

3.2.2.2.3.2.1. The veils obstructing the factors conducive to awakening

> The flaws are being unskilled with regard to the basis, laziness,
> the twofold impairment of samadhi,
> not generating, weakness,
> flaws pertaining to the view, and the negativities. (2.11)

The veils obstructing the close application of mindfulness[42] (factors 1–4), the subject, constitute *being unskilled with regard to the basis,* because they cause one to apprehend the four bases, such as the body, feelings, and so forth, in a mistaken way. It is mistaken because the body is apprehended as clean, feelings as happiness, the mind as the "self," and phenomena as "mine."

Laziness, the subject, is the veil obstructing the four perfect abandonments (factors 5–8),[43] because it opposes the abandonment of unwholesome factors that have already arisen, the prevention of unwholesome factors that have not been generated from arising, the generation of wholesome factors that have not yet arisen, and the increasing of the wholesome factors that have been generated.

The adverse conditions of sinking and agitation, and incomplete conducive factors such as intention, are the *two veils* obstructing the four causes of miraculous power (factors 8–12).[44] This is because they impair one's samadhi, which functions as the cause, due to which the resultant miraculous powers are not obtained. An alternative explanation is that the causes of miraculous power are obstructed by an incomplete presence of the four assisting factors, intention, and so on, and of the antidotes, which are the formative factors of abandonment. This is because these two factors impair one's samadhi, which in turn prevents the obtaining of the resultant miraculous powers.

Not generating faith and diligent perseverance, and so on, that is to say not applying oneself in cultivating faith and diligent perseverance, the subject, obstructs the five faculties (factors 13–17)[45] because it prevents the arising of the roots of wholesomeness conducive to liberation.[46]

When faith and the other four faculties are *weak,* the subject, the five powers (factors 18–22)[47] are obstructed, because they are too weak to overpower the opposing factors.

The factors abandoned by the path of seeing,[48] such as the *view* of the perishing collection and so on, the subject, obstruct the seven limbs of awakening (factors 23–29), because they prevent one from seeing reality directly.

The veil consisting of the *negativities,* the subject, obstructs the branches of the ārya path (factors 30–37), because it conflicts with the path of cultivation.[49]

The term *flaws* may be applied to each of the veils.

This completes the explanation of the veils obstructing the factors conducive to awakening.

3.2.2.2.3.2.2. The veils obstructing the pāramitās

> Veils obstructing affluence, pleasant rebirths,
> and not-abandoning sentient beings,
> decreasing faults and increasing positive qualities,
> and making others enter the path,
> acting for their liberation,
> inexhaustible and uninterrupted continuity of wholesomeness,
> bringing about certainty, enjoying the Dharma,
> and bringing to maturity. (2.12–13)

Miserliness, the subject, obstructs *giving* because it prevents one from obtaining a state of affluence (i.e., it obstructs one from becoming rich).[50]

Improper discipline, the subject, is termed the veil obstructing the pāramitā of *discipline* because it prevents one from attaining pleasant rebirths.

Anger, the subject, obstructs the pāramitā of *forbearance* because it prevents one from obtaining a state in which one never abandons sentient beings, a state that is based on forbearance.

Laziness, the subject, obstructs the pāramitā of *diligent perseverance* because it prevents one from decreasing faults and increasing positive qualities.

Distraction, the subject, is termed the veil that obstructs the pāramitā of *meditative stability* because it prevents one from using miraculous powers to bring those to be tamed on the path.

Improper wisdom, the subject, conflicts with the pāramitā of *wisdom* because it prevents one from working toward the liberation of those to be tamed.

To be without the wholesome qualities of the skillful means of awakening, the subject, conflicts with the pāramitā of *means* because it prevents the wholesome qualities from becoming inexhaustible.

Not engaging in aspirations, the subject, conflicts with the pāramitā of *aspiration* because it obstructs the uninterrupted continuity of the wholesome qualities.

A feeble capacity to overcome the factors adverse to the pāramitās, the subject, obstructs the pāramitā of *power* because it obstructs absolute certainty with regard to the results of the wholesome qualities.

To follow the literal meaning, the subject, conflicts with the pāramitā of *gnosis* or pristine wisdom because it prevents oneself and others from enjoying the profound Dharma and from bringing beings to maturity.

This completes the explanation of the veils obstructing the pāramitās.

3.2.2.2.3.2.3. The veils obstructing the grounds

> In order to realize the all-pervading, the supreme,
> the supreme purpose of the conducive cause,
> the absence of clinging,
> the absence of distinctions with regard to mental continua,
> the absence of affliction and purity,
> the absence of distinctions,
> the absence of decrease and increase,
> and the abode of the four masteries. (2.14–15)

Even though the natural purity of the dharmadhātu knows no distinctions of any kind, distinctions are made in terms of the ten grounds based on their specific ways of bringing about certainty in the post-attainment phases.[51] Based on these distinctions, ten veils are presented.

The manner of bringing about certainty during the post-attainment phases, which is based on the realization of the ultimate nature (*dharmatā*) attained in meditative equipoise, is presented as follows.

On the first ground, the dharmadhātu is realized as being *all-pervasive* during post-attainment. This realization is due to the strength of one's familiarization with the dharmadhātu [in meditative equipoise]. Thus, the meditative equipoise of the first ground serves that purpose.

During the post-attainment of the second ground one realizes that the cultivation of the dharmadhātu is the support for *increasingly perfecting* the realization of the dharmadhātu. Thus the meditative equipoise of the second ground serves that purpose.

Cultivating familiarity with the dharmadhātu on the third ground: during post-attainment there arises the realization that the study of the discourses, which is the *cause conducive* to the realization of the dharmadhātu, is the *supreme goal* to be pursued. Thus the meditative equipoise of the third ground serves that purpose.

Cultivating familiarity with the dharmadhātu on the fourth ground: during post-attainment one realizes the dharmadhātu *without clinging* to it as pertaining to a self in any way. Thus the meditative equipoise of the fourth ground serves that purpose.

Cultivating familiarity with the dharmadhātu on the fifth ground: during post-attainment one realizes that there are *no distinctions* with regard to the dharmadhātu of one's own and others' mental continua (i.e., they are identical in terms of their real nature). Thus the meditative equipoise of the fifth ground serves that purpose.

During the post-attainment of the sixth ground one realizes that the dharmadhātu is *neither previously totally afflicted, nor later completely purified.* Therefore, in order to generate this realization, one further cultivates familiarization with the dharmatā in meditative equipoise on the sixth ground.

During the post-attainment of the seventh ground, one realizes that the dharmadhātu of all phenomena has *no distinctions* insofar as it has no signs.[52] To generate this realization, the exaggeration that clings to signs with regard to the dharmadhātu is cut through in meditative equipoise.

During the post-attainment of the eighth ground, the dharmadhātu is realized as being *without increase and without decrease.* To achieve that realization, one places the mind in meditative equipoise in the mode of there being neither increase nor decrease in the dharmadhātu. On the eighth ground the dharmadhātu is realized as being without increase or decrease. This meditative equipoise, the subject, is referred to as the abode of the four masteries because it brings about the attainment of the excellent qualities of the four masteries over the nonconceptual, the fields, gnosis, and activities.

Q: How are these attained?

A: On the eighth ground arises mastery over nonconceptual gnosis and the completely purified fields because there is no more clinging to the signs of conceptual elaboration, and because one has obtained the power to display buddha fields and circles of retinues.

As a result of having cultivated familiarity with the dharmadhātu in meditative equipoise, one realizes during the post-attainment of the ninth ground that it (the dharmadhātu) is the *abode of the excellent qualities of mastery* over gnosis, because it brings about mastery over the four perfect discriminations.[53]

As a result of having cultivated familiarity with the dharmadhātu in meditative equipoise, one realizes during the post-attainment of the tenth ground that the dharmadhātu is the source of enlightened activities, because one now accomplishes the benefit of beings according to one's wishes.

These ten grounds are taught because cultivating familiarity with the dharmadhātu in meditative equipoise generates ten different ways of bringing about certainty during post-attainment. The dharmadhātu focused on during meditative equipoise is referred to as the support for the realizations attained during those ten phases. In the same way, the mind's dharmatā, which functions as the support for realization, is called spiritual disposition.[54]

> Ignorance with regard to the dharmadhātu
> consists of ten nonafflicted veils.
> The grounds themselves are the antidotes
> for that which conflicts with the ten grounds. (2.16)

Alternatively, the distinctive features of the means used to familiarize oneself with the dharmatā in meditative equipoise bring about those certainties in post-attainment. This is why the text mentions that each meditative equipoise "serves that [specific] purpose." Thus, the ten veils, which consist of nonafflicted ignorance[55] with regard to the dharmadhātu and so forth, are in conflict with the ten grounds. The antidotes that remove these veils are the ten grounds.

3.2.2.3. Summary

> All veils are taught as being included in
> the veil of afflictions and the cognitive veil.
> It is held that liberation is attained
> upon their exhaustion. (2.17)

All veils are said to be included in the veil of afflictions and the cognitive veil because there are no other veils apart from these two. All veils are included in these two because it is held that liberation from all veils is attained once these two are exhausted.

> These were the stanzas on the veils, the second chapter of *Distinguishing the Middle from the Extremes*.

This completes the explanation of the second chapter, the stanzas on the veils.

3.2.3. Explanation of the third chapter: Reality

3.2.3.1. Presentation of the main content

> Fundamental reality, reality in terms of its characteristics,
> the characteristics of the unmistaken,
> reality in terms of result and cause,
> coarse and subtle,
> generally known, the domain of purity,
> containing, differentiated characteristics,
> and reality in terms of expertise.
> These ten are the antidotes to the view pertaining to a self. (3.1–2)

Ten aspects of reality (*tattva; de kho na nyid*) are presented as the antidotes to the ten views relating to a self.

Q: What are these ten aspects?

A: Fundamental reality, reality in terms of its characteristics, unmistaken reality, reality in terms of result and cause, coarse and subtle reality, reality as it is generally known, reality that is the domain of purity, containing reality, reality in terms of its differentiated characteristics, and reality in terms of expertise.

The term *reality* refers to the way all phenomena really are, their mode of abiding (*gnas tshul*).

3.2.3.2. Detailed explanation of the branches

3.2.3.2.1. Fundamental reality

> The three natures are always nonexistent,
> existent but not real,
> and both really existent and nonexistent.
> These are held to be the three natures. (3.3)

Here, *fundamental reality* refers to the three natures.

Q: Why are they termed *fundamental*? Because these three contain everything.

Q: Why does one speak of *nature*? Because it is the way phenomena are.

Q: Why are they taught as threefold?

A: They are presented as three from the perspective of that which is to be discarded, that which is to be known, and that which is to be actualized. In other words, the imputed (that which is to be discarded) is the nature that never existed the way it was imagined. The dependent (that which is to be known) is the nature that exists substantially, and the perfected (that which is to be actualized) is the nature that is devoid of the duality of apprehended and apprehender.

Q: Why is the nature of things presented as threefold?

A: Of the three natures, the imputed is the nature that never existed the way it was imagined by the spiritually immature. The dependent is the nature that, although substantially existent, is not really as it appears. The perfected is the reality that consists of an existent nature and the nonexistence of the duality of apprehended and apprehender. In this way, the nature of things is held to be threefold.

This completes the explanation of fundamental reality.

3.2.3.2.2. Reality in terms of its characteristics

> Views of exaggeration and denial
> concerning phenomena and the individual,
> apprehended and apprehender,
> and existence and nonexistence
> do not occur when one understands
> the characteristics of reality. (3.4–3.5b)

In the context of the three natures, when the characteristics of reality in terms of the imputed nature are understood by means of study and contemplation, the views of exaggeration and denial do not occur.[56]

Q: In what way do exaggeration and denial not occur?

A: With a thorough understanding of the characteristics of the imputed, neither the view of exaggeration holding that phenomena and the individual are substantially existent nor the view denying their conventional existence occur.

When the characteristics of reality in terms of the dependent nature are understood by means of study and contemplation, exaggeration and denial do not occur.

Q: In what way do these views not occur with this knowledge?

A: With an understanding of the dependent, neither the view of exaggeration holding that both apprehended and apprehender exist substantially nor the view denying their conventional existence occur.

When the characteristics of reality in terms of the perfected nature are understood by means of study and contemplation, exaggeration and denial do not occur.

Q: In what way do exaggeration and denial not occur with this understanding?

A: With an understanding of the perfected, neither the view of exaggeration holding that apprehended and apprehender exist nor the view denying emptiness occur.

In other words, when the properties of the three natures are understood by means of study and contemplation, exaggeration and denial do not occur. This is reality in terms of its characteristics.

Q: Why do exaggeration and denial not occur with the understanding of the three natures?

A: With the understanding of the characteristics of the imputed, neither the view of exaggeration holding that phenomena and person are substantially existent nor the view denying their conventional existence occur. With the understanding of the characteristics of the dependent, neither the view of exaggeration holding that apprehended and apprehender are substantially existent nor the view denying their conventional existence occur. With the understanding of the characteristics of the perfected, neither the view of exaggeration holding that apprehended and apprehender are substantially existent nor the view denying emptiness occur.

3.2.3.2.3. Unmistaken reality

"Impermanent" refers to nonexistent things,
to objects with the characteristics of arising and perishing,
and to the change of stained to stainless.
These are applied to the three aspects of fundamental reality
   respectively. (3.5c–3.6b)

The unmistaken is taught as the antidote to the mistaken perception of clinging to things as permanent, pleasant, as self, and as mine ("I" and "mine").

Q: If all realities are included in fundamental reality, as stated above, then how are "impermanence" and so forth, which function as antidotes to mistaken perception, presented in this context? In other words, how do you present unmistaken reality within the context of fundamental reality?

A: Mistaken perception is the clinging to things as permanent, as pleasant, and so on. Unmistaken perception, on the other hand, refers to the antidotes of clinging to things as permanent and so on, consisting of the four aspects of the truth of suffering, namely impermanent, suffering, empty, and no-self.

The way to present them within the context of fundamental reality is as follows.

The term *impermanent* is applied to the three aspects of fundamental reality. It is used to refer to the imputed because it bears the meaning of "not being substantially existent," and because "permanent" means "existent at all times," which is the opposite of "impermanent."[57] The imputed, the subject, can be presented as impermanent because it bears the meaning of "being impermanent," and because it bears the meaning of "nonexistent," which is the opposite of "substantially existent at all times" or "permanent."

The dependent, the subject, is "impermanent" because it bears the characteristics of arising and perishing. The perfected, the subject, satisfies the criteria for being referred to by the conventional designation "impermanent," because it bears the meaning of "transformation from a stained into a stainless state."

The first of the three natures is termed "impermanent" from the perspective of bearing the meaning of the conventional designation "impermanent," the second from the perspective of the essential nature of impermanence, and the third from the perspective of having the temporal aspect of impermanence.

> **Because it brings about suffering, and by definition;**
> **by association is held to be different. (3.6cd)**

The characteristics of suffering are presented in the context of the sequence of the three aspects of fundamental reality in the following way.

The characteristics of suffering can be used to present the imputed, because by holding to the imputed as a real entity, one brings about all kinds of suffering. The dependent is suffering by definition, as it possesses the nature of the three types of suffering.[58] The perfected is suffering by association, because it is connected to suffering, suffering being that which bears the property (that is the perfected).[59] "Suffering by association" is held to be different from the previous two.

> **Reality is held to be empty because of nonexistence,**
> **not being the entity, and by nature. (3.7ab)**

The characteristics of emptiness can be applied to the three aspects of fundamental reality. The imputed is emptiness because it is nonexistent. The dependent is emptiness because it is the nature of that nonexistence. The perfected is held to be naturally empty. There are thus three types of emptiness: emptiness in terms of nonexistence, emptiness in terms of not being that nonexistence,[60] and emptiness by nature.

> **Reality is taught as being selfless due to being devoid of**
> **characteristics,**
> **because it has characteristics that are incompatible with it,**
> **and by virtue of its own characteristics. (3.7c–3.8a)**

The characteristics of selflessness are applied to the three aspects of fundamental reality.

The imputed is selfless because it is devoid of characteristics. The dependent is selfless because its characteristics are incompatible with those of the imputed. The perfected is selfless by virtue of its own characteristics. "Selflessness" is thus taught as being threefold.

3.2.3.2.4. Reality in terms of result and cause

Reality in terms of result and cause relates to the four truths.

3.2.3.2.4.1. The truth of suffering presented in terms of fundamental reality

It is therefore accepted as the truth of suffering. (3.8b)

It is appropriate to present the truth of suffering in terms of the three natures because the characteristics of suffering can be established in terms of the three natures.[61]

3.2.3.2.4.2. The truth of origination presented in terms of the three aspects of reality

Similarly, latencies, source,
and non-separation. (3.8cd)

Just as selflessness is divided into three aspects, origination too is presented as threefold, namely origination in the sense of latencies, origination in the sense of the source, and origination in the sense of non-separation.

The imputed satisfies the criteria for being referred to as origination in the sense of latencies because obsessive clinging to the imputed places the latencies of afflictions and conceptual thinking in the all-base. The dependent is referred to as origination in the sense of the source because it brings about the tainted skandhas. The perfected, the subject, is origination in the sense of non-separation because it is not separated from defilements, as is also the case with the suchness of origination, for instance.[62]

3.2.3.2.4.3. The truth of cessation presented in terms of fundamental reality

Due to its nature, the nonarising of the two,
and the pacification of defilements, which is held to be twofold.
(3.9ab)

There is cessation in terms of nonarising due to its nature, cessation in terms of nonarising of apprehended and apprehender, and cessation in terms of the pacification of defilements. Here, the basis for cessation is accepted as being twofold from the perspectives of suchness and of the freedom from stains.

Here, cessation in terms of nonarising due to its nature is the imputed, because there is no arising (with regard to the imputed) due to its very nature. Cessation in terms of nonarising of apprehended and apprehender is the dependent, because, being empty of both apprehended and apprehender, these two do not arise. The pacification of defilements is the perfected because it is suchness, and the cessation based on individual analysis.

3.2.3.2.4.4. The truth of the path presented in terms of fundamental reality

> Because it is to be thoroughly understood, abandoned,
> attained and actualized.
> This is an authentic explanation of the truth of the path.
> (3.9c–3.10a)

The imputed is termed "path," because it is to be thoroughly understood by means of the path. In this case, the object (the imputed) is given the name of that which holds the object (the path). The dependent is designated "path" because it is that which is to be eliminated by means of the path.[63] Here, the term "path" is given to the antidote. The perfected is labeled "path" because it is the truth of cessation to be attained by means of the path and the suchness that is to be actualized. Thus the truth of the path is authentically explained on the basis of the three natures.

3.2.3.2.5. Coarse and subtle reality

3.2.3.2.5.1. The coarse: divisions of the conventional

> Imputation, cognition,
> and expression are coarse. (3.10bc)

The conventional is threefold: the imputed conventional, the cognized conventional, and the conventional that is expression. All three are to be classified as "coarse reality" because they are the objects of cognition of a mind that is not in meditative equipoise.

The imputed conventional is the imputed, the cognized conventional is the dependent, and the conventional that is expression refers to the perfected in the sense that it captures the abstract notion of the ultimate nature (*dharmatā; chos nyid*).[64]

3.2.3.2.5.2. The subtle: divisions of the ultimate

The ultimate is only one. (3.10d)

The subtle, which is the actual ultimate,[65] refers to the perfected only and not to the other two characteristics.

> Object, attainment, and practice:
> these are held to be the three aspects of the ultimate.
> Unchanging and unmistaken
> are the two aspects of the perfected. (3.11)

The ultimate can be divided into three aspects: the ultimate object, the ultimate attainment, and the ultimate practice. These are the three aspects the ultimate is asserted to have. The ultimate object is suchness, because it is the domain of supreme gnosis. The ultimate attainment is nirvana, because it is the supreme goal to be attained. The ultimate practice is the path, because it is the supreme means to accomplish liberation.

The perfected has two aspects, the unchanging perfected and the unmistaken perfected.[66]

3.2.3.2.6. Reality as it is generally known

> One establishes worldly general knowledge,
> and three establish the general knowledge based on reasoning.
> (3.12ab)

Q: How is reality as it is generally known presented in terms of fundamental reality?

A: General knowledge is of two kinds: worldly general knowledge and general knowledge based on reasoning.[67] Worldly general knowledge is established from the perspective of the imputed nature alone, while worldly conventions are established by means of the intellect using signs.

General knowledge based on reasoning is established by means of direct perception, scripture, and inference.[68] Of these, the dependent is composed of direct perception and inference. The ultimate nature of these is contained in the perfected.

3.2.3.2.7. Reality in terms of the domain of purity

> Both aspects of the domain of purity
> are said to pertain to one nature alone. (3.12cd)

Reality in terms of the domain of purity is twofold: the domain of the gnosis purified of afflictions and the domain of the gnosis purified of the cognitive veils. It must be said that both exclusively pertain to the perfected only, it alone being the domain of gnosis, while the other two natures are not.

3.2.3.2.8. Containing reality

> Cause, conceptual thought,
> and name are contained in two natures;
> Genuine gnosis and superior reality
> are contained in one alone. (3.13)

This section teaches how five entities[69] are contained in fundamental reality. Of these five entities, cause, conceptual thought, and name are contained in the two aspects of the imputed and the dependent. Cause and conceptual thought are contained in the dependent and name in the imputed. Genuine gnosis and suchness, which is superior to the other categories mentioned above,[70] are both exclusively contained in the perfected.

3.2.3.2.9. Reality in terms of its differentiated characteristics

> The reality of involvement has two aspects,
> as have abiding and distorted engagement.
> Characteristics, cognition, purification,
> and genuine engagement all pertain to one nature only. (3.14)

Seven differentiated characteristics of reality are taught: the reality of involvement, of characteristics, of cognition, of abiding, of wrong engagement, of purification, and of genuine engagement. Those are explained in the *Sutra Unraveling the Intent* (*Saṃdhinirmocanasūtra; dgongs pa nges 'grel*).[71]

The *reality of involvement* is contained in the imputed and the dependent.[72] *Abiding*[73] and *distorted engagement* are contained in the dependent and the imputed, because their distinct existence is based on causes and conditions, and because they are objects of imagination.

The *reality of characteristics, cognition, purification,* and *genuine engagement* are contained in the perfected alone, because the reality of characteristics and the reality of purification are both contained in the unchanging perfected, and the remaining two (i.e., cognition and genuine practice) in the unmistaken perfected.

3.2.3.2.10. Reality in terms of expertise

Reality in terms of expertise has three divisions: the explanation of that which is to be discarded (i.e., the belief in a self), the antidotes expressed in terms of the three natures, and the explanation of expertise in the antidotes.

3.2.3.2.10.1. Explanation of the belief in a self

Unity, cause, consumer,
agent, controller,
in the sense of an owner, permanent,
the basis for affliction and purification,
practitioner, unfree then liberated:
these are the views pertaining to a self. (3.15–16ab)

The apprehension of the skandhas as a *singular unit* is the belief in a self that is to be discarded through expertise in the skandhas.

The apprehension of the eyes and so on (i.e., the eighteen elements of perception) as the self, and the subsequent clinging to it as the *cause* for experience is the belief in a self that is to be discarded through expertise in the elements of perception (*dhātu; khams*).

The apprehension of the sources of perception as the *consumer* is the belief in a self that is to be discarded through expertise in the sources of perception (*āyatana; skye mched*).

The apprehension of a self as the *agent* of all good and bad deeds is the belief in a self that is to be discarded through expertise in dependent arising.

The apprehension of a self as the one being in *control* is the belief in a self that is to be discarded through expertise in that which definitely occurs and that which cannot.[74]

The apprehension of a self in the sense of being an *owner* is the belief in a self that is to be discarded through expertise in the faculties.

The apprehension of a self as *permanent* is the belief in a self that is to be discarded through expertise in time.

The apprehension of a self as the *basis for total affliction and complete purification* is the belief in a self that is to be discarded through expertise in the ārya truths.

The apprehension of a self as the *practitioner* is the belief in a self that is to be discarded through expertise in the vehicles.

The apprehension of a self *being previously unfree and later liberated*[75] is the belief in a self that is to be discarded through expertise in the compounded and the uncompounded.

The views that create a self with regard to these ten objects are beliefs in a self which are to be discarded.

3.2.3.2.10.2. Expressing the antidotes in terms of the three natures

These antidotes are expressed here
in terms of imagination, conceptual thought, and real nature. (3.16cd)

Of the five skandhas,[76] the skandha of form is threefold: form imputed by imagination, form differentiated by conceptual thought, and form in the sense of its real nature.[77] Just as the three aspects of the form skandha correspond to the three natures, the other skandhas, the elements of perception, the sources of perception, and so forth (i.e., the antidotes mentioned above) must be understood in the same way.

3.2.3.2.10.3. Explanation of expertise in the antidotes

This explanation of the topics of expertise includes an explanation of the skandhas, the elements and sources of perception, dependent arising, that which definitely occurs and that which cannot, the faculties, the three times, the ārya truths, the three vehicles, and the compounded and the uncompounded.

We shall begin with the explanation of:

3.2.3.2.10.3.1. The meaning of the skandhas

> First, [skandha] means a multiplicity,
> collection, and complete distinction. (3.17ab)

The term "skandha" has three meanings: an assemblage of many things, containing everything, and complete distinction. In the first sense, the skandha of form is said to refer to an assemblage of many forms. In the second sense, the skandha of form is said to mean that this entity subsumes all forms. In the third sense, it is used to separately present each skandha after having distinguished them individually, such as form, feeling, and so on.

3.2.3.2.10.3.2. Explanation of the elements of perception

> The seeds of the apprehender, the apprehended,
> and of apprehending that object, are held to be different. (3.17cd)

The seeds of the apprehender is held to refer to the elements of the sense faculties such as the eyes and so on. *The seeds of the apprehended* is held to refer to the elements of the objects such as form and so on. *The seeds of apprehending the various objects,* form and so forth, refers to the elements of the consciousnesses, such as visual consciousness and so forth. The faculties and objects presented here are held to be different from the faculties and objects presented in the context of the sources of perception.[78]

3.2.3.2.10.3.3. Explanation of the sources of perception

> The gateway for the experience of sensations
> and of clearly determined objects is a different field of expertise.
> (3.18ab)

The six inner faculties of the eyes and so forth, the subject, are termed *sources of perception* because they are the gateway for the experience of sensations to arise. The six objects, form and so forth, the subject, are termed *sources of perception* because they are the gateway for a clearly determined experience[79] to arise from the various objects such as form and so on. The *experience* is consciousness. *Gateway for experience* means sources of perception, which is different from the two fields of expertise explained above (i.e., skandhas and elements).

3.2.3.2.10.3.4. Explanation of dependent arising

> No exaggeration and no denial
> with regard to cause, result, and effort. (3.18cd)

By penetrating the meaning of *dependent arising*, exaggeration and denial with regard to cause, result, and effort or activity are removed.

Exaggeration with regard to a cause means, in this context, that after giving up the idea of a creative cause, one conceives of a principal entity as a cause.[80] Denial in this context would be to think that there are no causes.

Exaggeration with regard to a result means thinking that happiness and suffering, and so on, come from the self or a principal entity, and so forth, while denial would be to think that results do not exist.

Exaggeration with regard to activity means thinking that happiness and suffering, and so on, come from the activity of a principal entity and so forth. Denial in this context refers to the idea that happiness and suffering, and so on, do not arise from good and bad actions respectively.

3.2.3.2.10.3.5. Explanation of that which definitely occurs and that which cannot

> Undesired, desired, purity,
> simultaneous occurrence, sovereignty,
> attainment, and conduct:
> these teach the meaning of dependency, another field of expertise. (3.19)

This topic is taught by means of seven dependent relationships. The dependent nature of *that which is undesired* refers to the fact that even though it is undesired, negative conduct brings about rebirth in an evil realm. The dependent nature of *that which is desired* is, for example, to be born in a pleasant realm by the power of one's good conduct. The dependent nature of *purity* is exemplified by the fact that purity is not obtained without eliminating the veils. The dependent nature of *simultaneous occurrence* is exemplified by the fact that two buddhas do not appear simultaneously in the same world, due to their karma of being peerless. The dependent nature of *sovereignty* is exemplified by the fact that with a female body one cannot exercise sovereignty over the seven possessions of a *cakravartin* universal emperor[81] such as the precious wheel and so forth. The dependent nature of *attainment* is exemplified by the fact that one does not obtain pratyekabuddhahood or buddhahood with a female body.[82] The dependent nature of *conduct* is exemplified by the fact that āryas do not commit actions such as killing and so forth. Those seven teach the meaning of dependent relationships, which is a field of expertise different from the ones mentioned above.

3.2.3.2.10.3.6. Explanation of the twenty-two faculties

> Because of apprehension, remaining, uninterrupted continuity, experience, and the two types of purity. (3.20ab)

The six sense faculties, from the eyes up to the mind (1–6),[83] the subject, are faculties because they control the production of the consciousnesses that apprehend their respective objects.

Life force (7), the subject, is a faculty because it controls remaining in existence in one particular type of birth.

The male and female sex organs (8–9), the subject, are faculties because they control the uninterrupted continuity of birth from a womb.

The five sensations (10–14), from pleasant to neutral,[84] the subject, are faculties because they control the experience of the result of wholesome and negative actions.

The five faculties from faith to wisdom (15–19), the subject, are faculties because they control worldly purity.[85]

The faculty that brings about the understanding of everything, the faculty of understanding everything, and the faculty of possessing the understanding of everything[86] (20–22) are faculties because they control the attainment of purity that is beyond the world.

In this way, the eight faculties of complete purity[87] are faculties because they control both worldly purity and the purity that is beyond the world.

3.2.3.2.10.3.7. Explanation of time

> To understand time in terms of result and cause,
> whether they are completed, or not yet completed,
> is another field of expertise. (3.20cd)

When both the result and the cause of a given phenomenon are completed, one speaks of "the past." The cause as completed means that the result has been brought about. The result as completed means that the result has been experienced and is exhausted. When the cause has been completed, but not yet the result, one speaks of "the present." In line with this explanation of the meaning of past and present, the meaning of "future" is that neither the cause nor the result are completed. This is the meaning of "time," which is a field of expertise different from the previous ones.

3.2.3.2.10.3.8. Explanation of the truths

> Sensation along with its cause,
> the cause of these, which is that which brings them about,
> the pacification thereof, and the antidote:
> this is asserted to be another field of expertise. (3.21)[88]

Tainted sensations along with their causes constitute the truth of suffering. The cause of this suffering, which is karma and affliction, is the truth of origination because it brings about rebirth. The pacification of both suffering and origination is the truth of cessation. The antidote for both suffering and origination is the truth of the path. These are asserted to be the four truths, yet another field of expertise.

3.2.3.2.10.3.9. Explanation of the three vehicles

> Excellent qualities, faults, and not conceptualizing:
> by understanding these, with the help of others or by oneself,
> for the sake of definite emergence—this is another field of
>   expertise. (3.22abc)

The śrāvaka vehicle consists of definite emergence from samsara[89] arising from an understanding of the excellent qualities of nirvana and the faults of samsara generated after listening to a teacher. The pratyekabuddha vehicle consists of definite emergence from samsara induced by an understanding of the excellent qualities of nirvana and the faults of samsara generated by oneself, without relying on a teacher. The Mahayana consists of definite emergence induced by an understanding that the faults of samsara and the excellent qualities of nirvana are equal; they are not conceptualized as being different. An understanding of these points is another field of expertise called "the vehicles."

3.2.3.2.10.3.10. Explanation of the conditioned and the unconditioned

> The last field of expertise is explained
> on the basis of designations and causes,
> and that which bears the meaning of complete pacification.
>   (3.22def)

The conditioned refers to that which is differentiated on the basis of having imputed designations and productive causes.[90] *The unconditioned* refers to the complete pacification of designations, and of arising and ceasing. These two are the last of the ten objects of expertise one must thoroughly understand.

> These were the stanzas on reality, the third chapter of *Distinguishing the Middle from the Extremes*.

This completes the explanation of the third chapter, the stanzas on reality.

3.2.4. Explanation of the fourth chapter: Cultivation of the antidotes

This chapter teaches the cultivation of the antidotes, the stages of their arising, and the way the result is attained by applying them.

3.2.4.1. The cultivation of the antidotes

3.2.4.1.1. Extensive explanation

3.2.4.1.1.1. The path of accumulation

The antidotes of the first path comprise the cultivation of the close applications of mindfulness, the cultivation of the four perfect abandonments, and the cultivation of the causes of miraculous activity.

3.2.4.1.1.1.1. The four close applications of mindfulness

> The close applications of mindfulness are cultivated
> to engage in the four truths,
> in terms of negativity, the cause of craving,
> the basis, and not being deluded. (4.1)

Those who want to attain liberation must engage in the adoption and rejection related to the four ārya truths. Therefore, in order to engage with the four truths, one begins by cultivating the four close applications of mindfulness.

Q: How does one engage with the four truths based on the four close applications of mindfulness?

A: With the cultivation of close application of mindfulness of the body one engages with the truth of suffering, because one understands how to differentiate the body in terms of the suffering of that which is nothing but negativity.[91]

With the cultivation of close application of mindfulness of feelings one engages with the truth of the origin, because one comes to realize that feelings function as the cause of craving, which is the principal origin of suffering.

With the cultivation of close application of mindfulness of the mind one engages with the truth of cessation, because one understands that the mind, which is the basis for the belief in a self, is not the self. Being thus freed from the fear connected with the annihilation of the self, one engages in the actualization of cessation.

With the cultivation of close application of mindfulness of phenomena one engages with the truth of the path, because one is not deluded with regard to that which must be eliminated and the antidotes that function as the eliminating factors.

3.2.4.1.1.1.2. Cultivating the four perfect abandonments

All aspects of discordant factors and antidotes
having been perfectly understood,
the four aspects of diligent perseverance arise
in order to abandon [or generate] them. (4.2)

Having perfectly understood the discordant factors that must be eliminated and the eliminating antidotes in all their aspects, one abandons the discordant factors that have already arisen and one prevents those that have not yet arisen from arising. One also generates the antidotes that have not yet arisen and enhances those that have. The arising of these four aspects of diligent perseverance is called the *four perfect abandonments*.

3.2.4.1.1.1.3. The four causes of miraculous activity

This has three parts: identifying the samadhi of the four causes of miraculous activity; showing how it arises from the antidotes that eliminate the faults; and the explanation of the antidotes that eliminate the faults.

3.2.4.1.1.1.3.1. Identifying the samadhi of the four causes of miraculous activity

Steadiness and serviceability,
and everything aimed for will be accomplished. (4.3ab)

Having set out in the practice with diligent perseverance, one will eventually achieve one-pointed concentration, the mind thus being made serviceable. This is the nature of the samadhi of the four causes of miraculous activity.

With this support, everything aimed for will be accomplished, such as supernatural powers and so forth.[92] This is the function of this samadhi. These two lines of this stanza explain both the nature and the function of the samadhi.

This samadhi is taught as being fourfold due to the particular features of its supporting factors of intention, diligent perseverance, will, and analysis.

3.2.4.1.1.1.3.2. How the samadhi arises from the antidotes that eliminate the faults

> Samadhi arises from its cause, which consists of relying on
> the eight formative factors that eliminate the five faults. (4.3cd)

The samadhi of the four causes of miraculous activity arises from the cause, which consists of relying on the eight formative factors that eliminate the five faults.

> Laziness, forgetting the instructions,
> sinking and agitation,
> not applying, and applying:
> these are held to be the five faults. (4.4)

There are five faults to be abandoned: (1) laziness, (2) forgetting the instructions, (3) sinking and agitation, (4) not applying the antidotes to that which prevents the enhancement of samadhi, and (5) applying antidotes even though sinking and agitation have already been pacified.

Laziness and *forgetting the instructions* prevent one from applying oneself to the cultivation of samadhi. *Sinking and agitation, not applying the antidotes to that which prevents the enhancement of samadhi,* and *applying antidotes even though sinking and agitation have already been pacified* are obstructions to the actual practice.

These are held to be the five faults related to samadhi.

3.2.4.1.1.1.3.3. Explanation of the antidotes that abandon the faults

> The basis and that which is based on it,
> cause and result. (4.5ab)

There are eight formative factors that enable one to abandon the five faults.

Laziness is abandoned by means of four factors: (1) intention, (2) effort, (3) faith, and (4) pliancy.[93] In this context, *intention* is the basis for effort, and *effort* is based on intention. The cause of intention is *faith*, and *pliancy* is held to be the result of effort.

Not forgetting the point of reference,
noticing sinking and agitation,
applying antidotes in order to abandon them,
and, once they are pacified, to abide in the genuine state of
    samadhi. (4.5c–f)

The four remaining formative factors of abandonment are: (5) recollection, (6) awareness, (7) will, and (8) equanimity.

Recollection acts as the antidote to forgetting the instructions because it makes one remember the instructions, which are the point of reference, without forgetting them.

Awareness acts as the antidote to sinking and agitation because it notices the occurrence of sinking and agitation, which are the faults related to samadhi.

Will acts as the antidote to not applying the antidotes because it brings about their repeated application in order to overcome sinking and agitation.

Equanimity acts as the antidote to excessive effort in applying the antidotes at times when there is neither sinking nor agitation. This is because it brings the mind to abide in the genuine state of samadhi naturally once sinking and agitation are pacified.

3.2.4.1.1.2. Cultivating the path of joining

The factors conducive to liberation having been generated,
the five faculties determine intention and application,
not forgetting the focal object,
not proliferating, and differentiation. (4.6)

When the factors conducive to liberation have been fully generated, the path of joining arises.

The five faculties that are to be cultivated at that point are as follows:

1. *The faculty of faith*, which determines one's intention with regard to the cultivation and abandonment related to the four truths
2. *The faculty of diligent perseverance*, which determines one's application in the practice of cultivation and abandonment related to the four truths

3. *The faculty of recollection*, which determines one's ability to not forget the focal object
4. *The faculty of samadhi*, which determines the ability of the mind to not proliferate
5. *The faculty of wisdom*, which determines the differentiation of phenomena

> Because the opposing factors are weak,
> one has the powers. The later ones are the result. (4.7ab)

Further, five powers conducive to definite distinction (i.e., the path of seeing) are to be cultivated. These are the five faculties of faith and so on, which are termed *powers* when they can no longer be overpowered by their opposing factors. This happens when these factors are weak. In the sequence of these five faculties, faith and so on, the later ones result from the earlier ones.[94]

Establishing the faculties and powers as the factors concordant with definite distinction:

> The faculties and powers
> each relate to two stages concordant with definite distinction.
> (4.7cd)

Of the factors concordant with definite distinction, the five faculties are posited for heat and peak (i.e., the first two of the four stages), and the five powers for forbearance and the supreme dharma (i.e., the remaining two stages).

3.2.4.1.1.3. Cultivating the path of seeing

> The limb of the nature, the limb of the abode,
> the third is the limb of definite emergence,
> the fourth is the limb of beneficial qualities,
> and three limbs are devoid of afflictions.
> Of these three, one is taught as being the basis,
> one the abode, and one its very nature. (4.8a–4.9b)

Since the seven limbs of awakening arise on the path of seeing, they will be explained next.

Of these seven, from the limb of right mindfulness up to equanimity, (1) the *discrimination of phenomena* is the "limb of the nature," as it is the essential nature of awakening.

(2) *Mindfulness* is the "limb of the abode," as it brings forth the other limbs.

(3) *Diligent perseverance* is the "limb of definite emergence," as it causes one to go beyond the factors opposing awakening.

(4) *Joy* is the "limb of beneficial qualities," as it benefits both body and mind.

(5) *Pliancy*, (6) *samadhi*, and (7) *equanimity* are the "limbs devoid of afflictions." Of these three, pliancy is said to be the basis for ridding the mind of afflictions, samadhi the state devoid of afflictions, and equanimity the essential nature devoid of afflictions. Pliancy acts as the basis for abandoning the afflictions, samadhi produces the mental state or abode necessary for abandoning them, and equanimity is contained in the state free from afflictions.

3.2.4.1.1.4. Cultivating the path of cultivation

Explaining the eightfold ārya path:

> Causing ascertainment and understanding,
> three limbs instill trust in others,
> three function as antidotes to the discordant factors:
> these are the eight limbs of the path.
> Three are held to generate in others an awareness
> concerning one's view, discipline, and few material needs.
> The antidotes to the discordant factors
> relate to afflictions, secondary afflictions, and mastery. (4.9c–4.11ab)

The antidotes for the factors discordant with the path of cultivation are the eight limbs of the ārya path, from right view up to right samadhi.

(1) *Right view* is the limb that brings about ascertainment with regard to the object, because it brings about ascertainment by means of the wisdom of the post-attainment phases with regard to that which has been realized on the path of seeing.

(2) *Right thought* and (3) *right speech* are the limbs that bring about understanding; motivated by right thought one uses right speech to bring about

in others the understanding of that which has been ascertained in oneself by means of the view.

(3) *Right speech,* (4) *right action,* and (5) *right livelihood* are the limbs by means of which one instills trust in others. By means of speech, one generates in others the awareness that one possesses a pure view; with right action that one possesses pure discipline; and with right livelihood that one has few material needs.

The remaining three are the limbs of the antidotes for the discordant factors.

(6) *Right effort* produces the antidotes for the afflictions discarded by means of the path of cultivation; (7) *right samadhi* generates the antidotes for the secondary afflictions; and (8) *right mindfulness* produces the antidote for the veil to the meditative absorptions, which bring about mastery over such excellent qualities as the supernatural powers and so forth.

3.2.4.1.2. Summary

> In accord, yet mistaken;
> connected, but turned away;
> unmistaken and not connected to the mistaken:
> these are the cultivations. (4.11c–12b)

On the paths of accumulation and joining, the path is cultivated via the close applications of mindfulness and so forth. They are mistaken because on these stages one still clings to the abstract notion of selflessness as being the actual essential nature of selflessness. However, as they are in accord with the understanding gained through study and contemplation, they do accord with the unmistaken.

In the context of the paths of seeing and cultivation, the path is cultivated via the limbs of awakening and so forth. Due to one's direct perception of selflessness, one has turned away from the mistaken. However, as one is still hampered by veils, one is still connected to the mistaken.

Cultivation in the context of the path of no further training (i.e., the culmination of familiarization) is explained as follows. Because the essential nature of this path is to be nonmistaken and because the veils have been eliminated, one is no longer connected to the mistaken.

Incidentally, there is an explanation of how the bodhisattvas' manner of cultivating the antidote is particularly exalted:

> Due to the bodhisattvas' focal object,
> mental engagement, and attainment,
> their practice is particularly exalted. (4.12cde)

Bodhisattvas are superior to śrāvakas and pratyekabuddhas in three ways. (1) While śrāvakas and pratyekabuddhas focus on their own bodies and feelings, and so on, bodhisattvas cultivate the practice focusing on both their own and others' bodies and so on. (2) Śrāvakas and pratyekabuddhas mentally engage with signs such as the impermanence of the body, and meditate, whereas bodhisattvas engage their minds in a nonreferential manner (i.e., free of conceptual signs). (3) Śrāvakas and pratyekabuddhas cultivate the path in order to disconnect from the impure body and so forth, and to obtain a nirvana that is inferior to that sought by bodhisattvas. Bodhisattvas, on the other hand, practice neither to disconnect nor to not disconnect from the body, and so forth, but to obtain nonabiding nirvana.

3.2.4.2. Explanation of the stages of the cultivation of the antidotes

This section contains an explanation of the eighteen stages and a summary.

3.2.4.2.1. Eighteen stages

> The causal stage, the stages of entering,
> joining, the one referred to as fruition,
> with activity and without, distinct,
> superior and unsurpassed. (4.13)

Identifying the particularities of each stage of the cultivation of antidotes:
(1) *The causal stage* refers to the individual with his or her particular spiritual disposition. (2) *The stage of entering the path* refers to the individual who generates the resolve to attain awakening in any of the three vehicles.[95] (3) *The stage of joining* begins with the generation of the resolve and lasts until one reaches the path of seeing. (4) *The stage of fruition* refers to the attainment of the first fruition (the path of seeing).[96] (5) *The stage with activity* is the path of training (the path of cultivation). (6) *The stage devoid of activity* is the path of no further training. (7) *The stage with distinctive features* is endowed with special qualities, such as the supernatural powers and so forth. (8) *The superior stage* refers to the bodhisattvas on any of the grounds.

(9) *The unsurpassed stage* is complete buddhahood, because there are no further stages beyond this.

> Conviction, engagement,
> definite emergence and prophecy,
> utterance and empowerment,
> culmination,[97] beneficial qualities,
> and a display of accomplishing activities. (4.14–4.15a)

(10) *The stage of conviction* is the ground of convinced conduct, which refers to the paths of accumulation and joining.[98] (11) *The stage of engagement* is the first ground. (12) *The stage of definite emergence* refers to grounds two through seven, because the bodhisattva traverses these grounds until their culmination by means of exerting effort. (13) *The stage of prophecy* is the eighth ground, as a buddha directly gives a prophecy to the bodhisattva at this point. (14) *The stage of utterance* is the ninth ground, because the bodhisattva, with a mind that perfectly knows to discriminate (*pratisaṃvid; so so yang dag par rig pa*), teaches the Dharma to those to be trained.[99] (15) *The stage of empowerment* is the tenth stage. On this stage a buddha bestows empowerment with an immense radiation of light.[100] (16) *The stage of culmination* is the attainment of the dharmakāya, because it is the culmination of realization. (17) *The stage of beneficial qualities* is the attainment of the saṃbhogakāya, because one experiences the joy and bliss of the Dharma in the company of bodhisattvas. (18) *The stage of displaying activities* is the attainment of the nirmāṇakāya, because one accomplishes activities for those to be trained by means of enlightened deeds.

3.2.4.2.2. Summary

> The dharmadhātu has three aspects:
> impure, partially purified,
> and completely purified.
> It is held that individuals
> can be appropriately classified through these. (4.15b–16b)

After differentiating three phases with regard to the dharmadhātu—impure, partially purified, and completely purified—the treatise explains how different kinds of individuals abiding on the above-mentioned stages are appropriately classified according to these three phases.

"Individuals on the impure stage" refers to those abiding on the causal stage, as well as those on the stages of entering, joining, and conviction. The "partially purified stage" refers to those who abide on the following eight stages: the stages of fruition, with activity, the superior stage, and the five stages from engagement to empowerment. "Those abiding on the thoroughly purified stage" refers to the stage devoid of activity, the stage with distinctive features, and the other remaining stages.

Alternatively, the phase in which the dharmadhātu is impure due to the stains refers to four types of individuals: those abiding on the causal stage and those abiding on the stages of entering, joining, and conviction. The phase in which the dharmadhātu is still impure due to having some of the stains, but already partially purified, refers to eight types of individuals: those abiding on the three stages of fruition and so forth, and those abiding on the five stages from engagement to empowerment. The phase in which the dharmadhātu is thoroughly purified of stains is held to refer to six types of individuals: those on the stage devoid of activity, those on the stage with distinctive features, and the others.

3.2.4.3. How the results are achieved based on the antidotes

3.2.4.3.1. Explanation of the five results

> Having become an eligible recipient is referred to as the fully
> ripened result,
> the power that results from this,
> longing, increase, and complete purification:
> these are the results in sequence. (4.16c–4.17b)

The five points, such as having become an eligible recipient and so forth, are explained by applying them to the five results respectively.[101]

Having become an eligible recipient for that which is wholesome is referred to as the *fully ripened result* (vipākaphala; rnam smin gyi 'bras bu), which is a body that has become an eligible recipient for the arising of wholesome qualities.

To possess the power to act in wholesome ways is the *dominant result* (*adhipatiphala; bdag po'i 'bras bu*), because one possesses the power to discard the opposing factors by virtue of having become an eligible recipient.

Deep longing for that which is wholesome is the *result similar to the cause* (*niṣyandaphala; rgyu mthun gyi 'bras bu*), because one wishes to act in wholesome ways due to the strength of having familiarized oneself in the past with that which is wholesome.

The increase in wholesome qualities is the *result of a person's deeds* (*puruṣakāraphala; skyes bu byed pa'i 'bras bu*), because the wholesome qualities develop in an unprecedented way through the power of familiarizing oneself with wholesome ways in the present.

Complete purification of the opposing factors is the *result of separation* (*visaṁyogaphala; bral ba'i 'bras bu*), because it is the state of complete distinctiveness that results from having discarded the veils.

3.2.4.3.2. Explanation of further types of result

> Successive, initial,
> familiarization and completion, (4.17cd)
> concordant and [separating from] the opposing factors,
> separate and distinct,
> superior and unsurpassed:
> these are, in brief, the other results. (4.18)

Successive results: based on one's spiritual disposition, one generates the resolve to attain awakening, based on which one engages in the path, which in turn gives rise to a result. Here, the earlier stages in turn give rise to the corresponding later results.

The *initial result* is the arising of the path of seeing, as it is the first attainment of states that are beyond worldly ones.

The *result of familiarization* refers to one's potential to achieve awakening becoming increasingly refined due to one's continuous familiarization with the earlier paths.

The *result of completion* refers to the perfection of abandonment and realization.

The *concordant result* arises in concordance with its cause, such as the generation of the resolve to attain one of the three types of awakening, which arises from one's spiritual disposition.

The *result that separates from the opposing factors* is the path of abandonment, as this is what separates one from the opposing factors.

The *result of separation* refers to both the result of familiarization and the result of completion, the former being the result belonging to the stage of training, and the latter the result belonging to the stage of no further training.

The *distinct result* refers to the supernatural powers and so forth.

The *superior result* refers to the bodhisattva grounds, because they are superior to the grounds of the śrāvakas and pratyekabuddhas.

The *unsurpassed result* is the buddha ground, as there are no other grounds above it.

This was the presentation of the further types of results, which completes the brief presentation of the results. Explaining this in detail is inconceivable.

> **These were the stanzas on the cultivation of the antidotes, the fourth chapter of *Distinguishing the Middle from the Extremes*.**

This completes the explanation of the fourth chapter, the stanzas on the cultivation of the antidotes.

3.2.5. Explanation of the fifth chapter: The unsurpassed vehicle

3.2.5.1. General presentation

> Its unsurpassed nature is held to be shown by
> its practice, its focal objects,
> and its genuine accomplishments. (5.1a–c)

Its unsurpassed practice, unsurpassed focal objects,[102] and its unsurpassed genuine accomplishments are held to show its unsurpassed nature.

3.2.5.2. Specific explanations

3.2.5.2.1. Unsurpassed practice

3.2.5.2.1.1. The six divisions of practice

> The practices have six aspects related to the pāramitās:
> supreme, mental engagement, concordant factors, abandoning
>   the extremes,
> specific, and general. (5.1d–5.2c)

The six aspects of the practice related to the six pāramitās are supreme practice, the practice of mental engagement, the practice of concordant factors, the practice of abandoning the two extremes, the specific practices, and the general practice.

3.2.5.2.1.2. The individual nature of the six aspects

3.2.5.2.1.2.1. The supreme practice

3.2.5.2.1.2.1.1. The nature of the twelve supreme aspects

> The nature of the practice has twelve supreme aspects.
> These are held to consist of
> supreme vastness, duration,
> purpose, inexhaustibility,
> uninterrupted continuity, freedom from hardships,
> mastery, being perfectly embraced,
> beginning, attainment, concordance with the cause, and accom-
>   plishment. (5.2d–5.4b)

Q: What are the twelve supreme aspects of the practice?

A: (1) The practice is supreme in its *vastness,* as it leads to vast qualities that lie beyond this world. (2) It is supreme in its *duration,* as one diligently exerts oneself in the six pāramitās over a period of three immeasurable eons. (3) It is supreme in its *purpose,* as the practices of giving and so on are accomplished for the benefit of all sentient beings. (4) It is supreme in its *inexhaustibility*, as by dedicating the wholesome force of giving and the other pāramitās to great awakening, it becomes inexhaustible even in the state without remainder. (5) The practice is supreme in its *uninterrupted continuity*, as the wholesomeness of giving and the other pāramitās are made to continue without interruption. (6) It is supreme in being *free from hardships*, as the skillful means of rejoicing increases one's practice of giving and so forth. (7) It is also supreme in terms of *mastery*, as it brings control over the treasury of space.[103] (8) The practice is supreme in terms of *being perfectly embraced*, as the practices of giving and so forth are accomplished in the manner of being embraced by nonconceptual gnosis. (9) Supreme *beginning* means that one's realization of selflessness increases more and more on the paths of accumulation and joining. (10) It is supreme in terms of *attainment*, as the path that is beyond the world is attained for the first time on the first ground. (11) Its *concordance with the cause* is supreme, as the causes concordant with the six pāramitās arise sequentially from the second to the ninth grounds. (12) The *accomplishment* is supreme, as one accomplishes the ultimate excellent qualities by completing the bodhisattvas' activities on the tenth ground.

These are held to be the twelve supreme aspects of the practice.

3.2.5.2.1.2.1.2. Condensing the twelve supreme aspects into the ten pāramitās

> Thus, due to their supreme characteristics,
> they are held to be the ten pāramitās. (5.4cd)
> Giving, ethical discipline, forbearance, and diligent
>   perseverance,
> meditative concentration, wisdom, and skillful means,
> aspiration, power, and gnosis:
> these are the ten pāramitās. (5.5)

Being endowed with these twelve supreme aspects, these practices are called pāramitās precisely because they are supreme.[104] It is asserted that there are ten distinct pāramitās: giving, ethical discipline, forbearance, diligent perseverance, meditative concentration, wisdom, skillful means, aspiration, power, and gnosis.

3.2.5.2.1.2.1.3. The functions of the ten pāramitās

> Their functions are to take under one's care,
> not to harm, to tolerate,
> to increase the excellent qualities, to enable one to bring others
>   to the Dharma,
> to liberate,
> to render inexhaustible, to engage at all times,
> to ensure, to delight and to bring to maturity. (5.6)

The ten pāramitās have the following functions.

By practicing *giving* one satisfies others and takes them under one's care.

Due to *ethical discipline* one does not harm others because it eliminates all harm along with its basis.[105]

Forbearance enables one to tolerate any suffering and harm caused by others.

Diligent perseverance increases the excellent qualities more and more.

Practicing *meditative concentration* enables one to bring those to be trained to the teachings by means of miraculous deeds.

With *wisdom* one liberates others' minds by teaching them the Dharma.

With expertise in *skillful means* one renders one's wholesome qualities inexhaustible by dedicating them to great awakening.

Aspirations enable one to engage at all times in wholesome deeds by leading one to practice giving and the other pāramitās in all future lives.

Power makes certain that the wholesome qualities of giving and so forth lead to awakening by overpowering the opposing factors.

Gnosis makes one take delight in the Dharma, such as in the practice of giving and the like, and it brings beings to maturity.

3.2.5.2.1.2.2. The practice of mental engagement

3.2.5.2.1.2.2.1. The nature of mental engagement

3.2.5.2.1.2.2.1.1. The actual practice of mental engagement

> Bodhisattvas constantly engage their minds
> with the dharmas

as prescribed in the Mahayana
by means of three wisdoms. (5.7)

Bodhisattvas constantly engage their minds[106] with the dharmas of the Mahayana, and those of the sutras and melodic verses and so forth,[107] just as prescribed. And just as it is prescribed, they continuously keep these teachings in mind by means of the three wisdoms, which arise from repeated study, contemplation, and cultivation.

3.2.5.2.1.2.2.1.2. The benefits of mental engagement

They develop the element, penetrate,
and accomplish the aims. (5.8ab)

Engaging with the Dharma by means of the wisdom of study develops their spiritual element.[108] The wisdom that has arisen from contemplation enables them to penetrate the meaning of what they studied by relying on reasoning, and the wisdom that has arisen from cultivation brings about the accomplishment of the desired aims because it purifies the access to the bodhisattva grounds.

3.2.5.2.1.2.2.2. Classifying mental engagement into ten Dharma activities

3.2.5.2.1.2.2.2.1. The actual classification

One must know that it is
perfectly connected to ten Dharma activities:
writing, venerating, offering,
listening, reading, memorizing,
explaining, reciting out loud,
reflecting and meditating. (5.8c–5.9)

One should know that this mental engagement is perfectly accomplished in connection with ten Dharma activities.

Q: What are these ten?

A: They are (1) to write down the Mahayana teachings, (2) to venerate them, (3) to offer them to others, (4) to listen to them oneself, (5) to read the scriptures, (6) to memorize them, (7) to explain them to others, (8) to recite them out loud;[109] (9) to reflect on their meaning by means of the wisdom that has arisen from contemplation, and (10) to meditate on them by means of correct mental engagement.

3.2.5.2.1.2.2.2.2. The benefits

> The nature of these ten activities
> involves an unfathomable amount of merit,
> because they are superior, inexhaustible,
> benefit others, and do not end. (5.10)

The nature of these Dharma activities is such that their merit is unfathomable, one of them alone conveying a vast amount of merit.

Q: Of all the practices explained in the sutras, why are only the Mahayana Dharma activities taught as being particularly exalted?

A: Because (1) they are superior to the activities of the śrāvakas and so forth, (2) the kāyas and gnosis are not exhausted even in the expanse without remainder, (3) they cause the potential of enlightened activities to be incessantly active as long as samsara endures, and (4) they incessantly accomplish others' benefit.

3.2.5.2.1.2.3. The practice of concordant factors

3.2.5.2.1.2.3.1. General exposition

> The concordant factors are
> being undistracted and unmistaken. (5.11ab)

The practice of factors concordant with reality is twofold: the cultivation of calm abiding (being undistracted), and the cultivation of special insight (being unmistaken).

3.2.5.2.1.2.3.2. Specific explanations

3.2.5.2.1.2.3.2.1. Explanation of distraction, the factor discordant with calm abiding

> Wise ones should know distraction [to be of the following types]:
> emerging, engaging with objects,
> and likewise savoring the taste, sinking and agitation,
> a [mistaken] confidence,
> the thought of self-clinging,
> and a low mental attitude. (5.11c–5.12)

There are six types of distraction:

1. *Natural distraction* refers to the group of five consciousnesses, such as the eye consciousness and so forth, because the occurrence of any of the five sense consciousnesses causes one to emerge from the samadhi.

2. *External distraction* refers to the mental consciousness, because it diverts the mind's focus outside when the mental consciousness engages with objects.

3. *Inner distraction* refers to savoring the taste of samadhi, and to sinking and agitation, because these experiences reduce the quality of the inner samadhi.

4. *Distraction due to signs* refers to a [mistaken] confidence after apprehending the signs of practice in samadhi, because one confuses a state in which one has not obtained the excellent qualities with their attainment.

5. *Distraction due to negativities* is the thought that one is superior to others as a result of self-clinging, because it carries the signs of pride.

6. *Distraction of mental engagement* refers to a low or inferior mental attitude, because one is mentally engaged with the Hinayana.

Thus, having understood these six distractions, a wise individual should cultivate the state of calm abiding in which they are completely pacified.

3.2.5.2.1.2.3.2.2. Explanation of unmistaken knowing, the essence of special insight

3.2.5.2.1.2.3.2.2.1. The ten divisions of unmistaken knowing

> Syllables, actuality, mental engagement,
> nonproliferation, two characteristics,
> impurity and purity, adventitious,
> fearlessness and lack of arrogance. (5.13)

(1) Unmistaken with regard to syllables,[110] (2) unmistaken with regard to actuality (*artha; don*), (3) unmistaken with regard to mental engagement (*manasikāra; yid la byed pa*), (4) unmistaken with regard to nonproliferation, (5–6) unmistaken with regard to both particular and general characteristics, (7) unmistaken with regard to both impurity and purity, (8) unmistaken with regard to the adventitious, (9) unmistaken with regard to fearlessness, and (10) unmistaken with regard to the lack of arrogance.

3.2.5.2.1.2.3.2.2.2. The meaning of these ten divisions

Explanation of the meaning of the first of the ten types of unmistaken knowing:

3.2.5.2.1.2.3.2.2.2.1. Unmistaken with regard to syllables

> Due to connection and acquaintance, or
> due to a lack of connection and acquaintance,
> syllables have a meaning or do not.
> Knowing this, one is unmistaken with regard to syllables. (5.14)

Syllables perform their function when the syllables that make up words that correctly express a meaning are arranged in the right order, and when one is acquainted with the language consisting of those syllables. In the opposite case (i.e., when the syllables are not connected in the right way and one is not acquainted with the language), they do not perform their function. Knowing when syllables have meaning and when they do not is to engage with them in an unmistaken manner. From this understanding arises a realization in the bodhisattvas that is beyond that expressed by words.[111]

3.2.5.2.1.2.3.2.2.2.2. Unmistaken with regard to actuality

> That which appears as duality
> does not exist in this way.
> When one is unmistaken with regard to actuality,
> existence and nonexistence are discarded. (5.15)

Apprehended and apprehender appear in a dualistic manner. Since, in actuality, they do not exist the way they appear, the extreme of existence is discarded. Since it is not the case that mere dualistic appearances do not exist, the extreme of nonexistence is discarded. To know both is to be unmistaken with regard to actuality. From this understanding arises a realization free from the duality of apprehended and apprehender.

3.2.5.2.1.2.3.2.2.2.3. Unmistaken with regard to mental engagement

> The basis for mental engagement is conceptual thought
> tainted by that [dualistic] concept.
> Unmistaken with regard to mental engagement,
> one is aware of the cause of the dualistic appearances. (5.16)

Conceptual thought tainted by the concepts formed in the past that apprehend things in terms of apprehended and apprehender, the subject, is termed *basis for mental engagement,* because it is the support for the seeds of mental engagement. Knowing this is to be unmistaken with regard to mental engagement.

Q: What is this basis of mental engagement?

A: It is a name given to the all-base, which is the cause of the dualistic appearances of apprehended and apprehender.

3.2.5.2.1.2.3.2.2.2.4. Unmistaken with regard to nonproliferation

> Nonexistence and existence in actuality
> are held to be like a magical illusion and so forth.
> This understanding is unmistaken with regard to
>   nonproliferation,
> because it does not proliferate "existence" and "nonexistence."
>   (5.17)

That which actually exists is the dependent, and that which does not exist is the duality of apprehended and apprehender. Even though they do not actually exist, they are held to appear in the same way as magical and optical illusions do. The realization that although there are dualistic appearances on the conventional level, they do not exist in actuality, is the unmistaken understanding with regard to nonproliferation. This is because this realization does not proliferate concepts that cling one-sidedly to either "existence" or "nonexistence."

3.2.5.2.1.2.3.2.2.2.5. Unmistaken with regard to particular characteristics

> As no conceptual thought applies [to the real nature of things],
> everything exists only nominally.
> Knowing this, one is unmistaken with regard to the particular
> characteristics.
> This applies to the particular characteristics of the ultimate.
> (5.18)

All objects of knowledge, which are included in the twelve sources of perception, are only nominally existent. This is because the way they are apprehended by means of conceptual thought does not apply to their true nature. To know things in this way is to be unmistaken with regard to the particular characteristics.

Q: With regard to which characteristics is one unmistaken?

A: One is unmistaken with regard to the particular characteristics of the ultimate.

3.2.5.2.1.2.3.2.2.2.6. Unmistaken with regard to the general characteristic

> Apart from the dharmadhātu
> there are no phenomena as such.
> Therefore, this is what it means to be unmistaken
> with regard to this general characteristic. (5.19)

Since all phenomena are nothing but mere labels, there are no phenomena apart from the dharmadhātu (i.e., selflessness). Thus, all phenomena amount to nothing more than mere labels. Since all phenomena are devoid of a self, one is unmistaken with regard to the general characteristic when one knows that the general characteristic of phenomena is selflessness.

3.2.5.2.1.2.3.2.2.2.7. Unmistaken with regard to both impurity and purity

> Depending on whether or not
> mistaken mental engagement has been discarded,
> it (the dharmadhātu) is pure or impure.
> Knowing this, one is unmistaken with regard to that. (5.20)

As long as one has not discarded mistaken mental engagement, this dharmadhātu is impure. Once discarded, however, it is purified. To understand this is to be unmistaken with regard to both impurity and purity.

3.2.5.2.1.2.3.2.2.2.8. Unmistaken with regard to the adventitious

> As the dharmadhātu is by nature pure,
> it is like space;
> both occur adventitiously.
> Knowing this, one is unmistaken with regard to that. (5.21)

Both the earlier state associated with stains and the later state purified of stains arise adventitiously. This is because the stains that exist at the earlier impure stage are adventitious, and because the dharmadhātu is by nature pure, similar to space; and because at the later stage as well, when purified of stains, it is merely the purification of adventitious stains.[112] To understand this is to be unmistaken with regard to the adventitious.

3.2.5.2.1.2.3.2.2.2.9–10. Unmistaken with regard to fearlessness and lack of arrogance

> There is neither affliction nor purification
> of phenomena and individuals, because they do not exist.
> Therefore, there is neither fear nor pride.
> Knowing this, one is unmistaken with regard to that. (5.22)

Phenomena are neither essentially totally afflicted at the earlier stage, nor are they later purified. And neither is the nature of whatever is established as essentially totally afflicted purified at the later stage. This is because phenomena and individuals, the duality of apprehended and apprehender, do not exist in the ultimate sense. That being so, the bodhisattvas are not afraid of or terrified by the thought of their faults increasing, nor is there any pride in those who develop their excellent qualities. To understand this means in this context to be unmistaken with regard to fearlessness and lack of arrogance. This understanding brings about the realization that the dharmadhātu is devoid of exhaustion and increase.

In this way, the ten unmistaken understandings correspond to the ten vajra phrases. The ten vajra phrases mentioned in the sutras, such as, "existence and nonexistence," and so forth, are summarized in verse form in Vasubandhu's commentary:[113]

> Existence and nonexistence, unmistaken,
> the basis, like a magical illusion,
> nonconceptual, by nature permanent luminosity,
> total affliction and complete purification,
> space-like,
> without decrease, and without remainder:
> these are the ten vajra phrases.[114]

These vajra phrases may be related to the ten unmistaken understandings as follows:

(1) *Unmistaken with regard to syllables* corresponds to "existence and nonexistence," (2) *unmistaken with regard to actuality* corresponds to "unmistaken," (3) *unmistaken with regard to mental engagement* corresponds to "the basis," (4) *unmistaken with regard to nonproliferation into the two extremes* corresponds to "like a magical illusion," (5) *unmistaken with regard to the particular characteristics* corresponds to "nonconceptual," (6) *unmistaken with regard to the general characteristic* corresponds to "luminous by nature," (7) *unmistaken with regard to both impurity and purity* corresponds to "total affliction and complete purification," (8) *unmistaken with regard to adventitious occurrence* corresponds to "space-like," (9) *unmistaken with regard to not being terrified by the fact that the factors to be eliminated do not decrease [in strength or number]* corresponds to "without decrease," and (10) *unmis-*

taken with regard to the lack of arrogance based on the increasing power of the antidotes corresponds to "without superiority or remainder."

Just as it is difficult to break a physical vajra with some other weapon,[115] these phrases are difficult to understand. This is why they are called vajra phrases.

In his commentary, Vasubandhu expounds on this brief presentation of the vajra phrases in two ways. He first presents them in terms of "the three natures, the focal objects, nonconceptuality, and the objections and responses that consist of the remaining vajra phrases."[116]

The second explanation is as follows:

> With regard to what confusion is about, what it is, and why
>   there is confusion,
> what is non-confusion and what it is about,
> the results of confusion and non-confusion,
> and the limit of both.[117]

Here, the three natures are the focal objects: since "existence" is the perfected, "nonexistence," the imputed, and "unmistaken," the dependent, the three natures are that which is to be known.

Nonconceptual awareness is that which is unmistaken with regard to the particular characteristics. Luminosity is that which is known nonconceptually. This is a presentation of the objects to be known and the knower.

The remaining vajra phrases are taught by means of the objections and responses. They are explained as follows:

Objection: If the imputed and the dependent characteristics do not exist, how can they be focal objects? And if they do exist, then these phenomena cannot be naturally luminous.[118]

Response: This is explained by the resemblance to a magical illusion. Even though that which is created by magical illusion does not exist as it appears, it can still be observed.

Objection: Again, if phenomena are naturally luminous, how can they be totally afflicted at the earlier stage and purified later on?

Response: The dharmas of total affliction and complete purification must be understood to be like space. Space is naturally pure, and so is luminosity. In this way, one only speaks of "total affliction" and "complete purification" with regard to luminosity.

Objection: If there have been countless buddhas who have dispelled the afflictions of countless beings, then why doesn't samsara decrease [in terms of the number of sentient beings] and nirvana increase?

Response: This is explained by means of the phrases "without decrease" and "without superiority." Since sentient beings (i.e., the aspect of total affliction) and the factors of complete purification are limitless, samsara and nirvana are taught to be without decrease or increase.

The sequence of the vajra phrases taught here does not accord with the way they are presented in Vasubandhu's commentary.[119] The sequence here follows mainly the order of explanation. The text that teaches the ten vajra phrases is the topic to be explained, and the stanzas beginning with "With regard to what confusion is about, what it is, . . ." and so on, are the verses that elucidate them. Thus a connection between the earlier and later verses has been made.

3.2.5.2.1.2.4. The practice of abandoning dual extremes

> The extremes of being different or identical,
> those of non-Buddhist and Śrāvaka schools,
> the two extremes of exaggeration and denial
> with regard to both the individual and phenomena,
> the extremes of discordant factors and the antidotes,
> the notions of permanence and annihilation,
> apprehended and apprehender,
> the three aspects of both total affliction and complete
>   purification,
> and the extremes of dual conceptualizations:
> these are held to be the seven types of extremes. (5.23–5.25ab)

The practice consists of the path that enables one to understand in detail and to accomplish the middle way through relinquishing all dual extremes by means of discriminating wisdom.

[There are seven sets of two extremes:]

1. The first two extremes to be eliminated are the extremes imputed by both the non-Buddhist and the Śrāvaka schools.

Q: What are these extremes?

A: The imputations of the non-Buddhist schools are the extremes of imputing the self and the skandhas as either different or identical, as well as the imputation that form and so forth are permanent. To label phenomena as impermanent is the extreme imputed by the śrāvakas. These are the two extremes imputed by the non-Buddhist and the Śrāvaka schools.

2. The two extremes of exaggeration and denial with regard to the individual, and the two extremes of exaggeration and denial with regard to phenomena, are the four extremes.

3. There are also the two extremes of the discordant factors, ignorance and so forth, on the one hand, and the antidotes that bring ignorance to an end, on the other.

4. The extreme of permanence is the imputation created by the notion that both the individual and phenomena exist by virtue of an essential nature. The extreme of annihilation is the imputation created by the notion that they are conventionally nonexistent.

5. There are the two extremes of imputing phenomena as apprehended and apprehender.

6. There are the two extremes of the three total afflictions and of the three complete purifications. The three total afflictions are the afflictions of total affliction, the total affliction of karma, and the total affliction of birth. The three complete purifications are the three doors of liberation.[120] Clinging to them results in imputation, which is an extreme.

7. Conceptual thoughts related to the two aspects of substantial existence and nonexistence and so forth are also extremes.

These are held to be the seven types of dual extremes.

> Existence and nonexistence of the entity,
> that which is to be pacified and the pacifier,
> the object of fear and being afraid of it,
> apprehended and apprehender,
> the genuine and the mistaken,
> agent and inability,
> nonarising and coexistence:
> these are the extremes of dual conceptualizations. (5.25cd–5.26)

The following seven sets are the extremes of conceptualization related to the subject aspect of the two extremes:

1. The two extremes of conceiving the entity of the self as being either existent or nonexistent

2. The two extremes of conceptualization with regard to that which is to be pacified (i.e., the factors to be relinquished), and that which brings about their pacification (i.e., the antidotes)
3. The two extremes of the concepts that things are devoid of an essential nature, which is the object of one's fear, and the concept of being afraid of this emptiness
4. The concepts of apprehended and apprehender
5. The two extremes of conceptualization with regard to the untainted genuine state and the tainted mistaken state
6. The extremes of conceptualizing gnosis as being that which discards the factors to be relinquished on the one hand, and on the other hand, that the potential to discard them does not exist
7. The extremes of conceptualizing the nonarising of the antidotes, and that even if they have been generated, they coexist with the factors to be relinquished

3.2.5.2.1.2.5–6. The specific practice and general practice

The specific and the general
must be understood to relate to the ten grounds. (5.27ab)

Having understood that the pāramitās are to be accomplished in a pure way on the ten grounds, the *general practice* refers to the fact that there is no distinction with regard to the mere practice of the ten pāramitās on the ten grounds (i.e., all ten pāramitās are cultivated on each of the ten grounds). *Specific* refers to the fact that on each ground the practice of a specific pāramitā is predominant.

3.2.5.2.2. Unsurpassed focal objects

Exposition, the expanse of suchness,
that which is practiced, accomplishment, comprehension,
ascertainment, complete comprehension,
complete realization, supreme enhancement,
understanding, abiding in the genuine state,
and eminence: these are held to be the focal objects.
(5.27cd–5.28)

1. The basis[121] of *exposition* consists of the twelve branches of scriptures, because they are laid out to benefit sentient beings.

2. The focal object used to realize the dharmadhātu is dharmatā, because it is the *suchness* that is the focal object on the path.

3. The focal objects of the practice are the ten pāramitās, because they are *that which is to be practiced*.

4. The focal object for *accomplishment* is suchness, because the path is accomplished by focusing on suchness.

5. The focal object of *comprehension* is the object of the wisdom that has arisen from study, because it is that which is to be grasped by means of the wisdom of study.

6. The focal object of *ascertainment* is the object of the wisdom of contemplation, because it is ascertained based on reasoning.

7. The focal object of *complete comprehension* is the object of the wisdom of cultivation, because it is that which is to be apprehended by an individual self-knowing mind.

8. The focal object of *complete realization* is the focal object of the path of seeing on the first ground, because it is that which is to be realized by means of the path that is beyond the world.

9. The focal object of *supreme enhancement* is the focal object from the second up to the seventh ground, because it is the focal object for the enhancement of realization based on the earlier realization.

10. The focal object of *understanding* is the focal object of the seventh ground, because it is the deep penetration of the focal objects of both the worldly path and the path that is beyond the world.[122]

11. The focal object of abiding in the genuine state is the focal object of the eighth ground, because it is a focal object that is unmoved by conceptual thoughts that apprehend signs.[123]

12. The focal objects of the ninth, the tenth, and the buddha ground are held to be particularly eminent. On the ninth ground, one obtains the eminent gnosis of the four perfect discriminations,[124] on the tenth ground, the eminent power over action, and on the buddha ground, the eminent purity of having relinquished all veils without exception.

3.2.5.2.3. Unsurpassed genuine accomplishments

> **Nothing missing, not abandoning,**
> **not diverted, complete,**

genuine generation, increase,
serviceability, not remaining,
absence of veils, and unceasing:
these are the genuine accomplishments. (5.29)

There are ten unsurpassed genuine accomplishments:

1. The circumstance that there are *no conditions missing* for the path is the genuine accomplishment of the spiritual disposition.

2. *Not abandoning* the Mahayana is the genuine accomplishment of conviction.

3. *Not being diverted* toward the Hinayana is the genuine accomplishment of the resolve to attain buddhahood.

4. To have *completely* accomplished the pāramitās is the genuine accomplishment of the practice.

5. To *genuinely generate* the ārya path is the genuine accomplishment of entering the faultless.

6. To *increase* the roots of wholesomeness is the genuine accomplishment of bringing sentient beings to maturity.

7. Having made the mind *serviceable* is the genuine accomplishment of the complete purification of the field.

8. *Not remaining* in either samsara or nirvana is the genuine accomplishment of having received the prophecy.

9. The *absence of veils* is the genuine accomplishment of the buddha ground.

10. To *unceasingly* display awakening is the genuine accomplishment of the display of awakening, which refers to the display of the twelve great deeds of a buddha.

3.2.5.3. Explaining the greatness of and necessity for this treatise

The treatise that distinguishes the middle from the extremes
is difficult to understand, contains the essential purport,
is of great purpose, is of benefit to all,
and dispels everything that is of no value. (5.30)

The text taught here is the *Madhyāntavibhāga-śāstra, Distinguishing the Middle from the Extremes*. This treatise, the subject, is difficult to understand, as it is not the domain of mere intellectuals. Immune to argumentative objections and being the supreme domain of gnosis, it contains the essential purport of all Dharma teachings. This text serves a great purpose, because it teaches extensively the activities of the bodhisattvas who practice for the benefit of sentient beings. And just as it is of great benefit, it is of practical relevance for all three types of beings endowed with a spiritual disposition, because it teaches the path of the three vehicles. It eliminates everything that is of no value, because it eliminates both the afflictive and the cognitive veils.

> These were stanzas on the unsurpassed vehicle, the fifth chapter of *Distinguishing the Middle from the Extremes.*

This completes the explanation of the fifth chapter, the stanzas on the unsurpassed vehicle.

> This completes the stanzas of the treatise entitled *Distinguishing the Middle from the Extremes,* composed by Ārya Maitreya.

> It was translated, edited, and revised by the Indian preceptors Jinatra and Śīlendrabodhi, and the translator-editor Bande Yeshe De.

4
CONCLUDING VERSES AND
VERSES OF ASPIRATION

Your excellent speech, like a great snow mountain lake endowed with
    water's eight qualities,
adorned with sapphire clouds rich with an endless rain of fine
    explanations,
is the playground of the bodhisattvas, lords of nāgas,
an inexhaustible treasury of infinite wisdom.

The stainless moonlight of Ajita's excellent speech
is a gateway to distinguish the doctrines in groundbreaking ways,
offering fine explanations endowed with the supreme of all aspects,
moving the anthers of the pleasing, most amazing, and profound
    meaning.

Illuminating the smile of the jasmine flower of intelligence,
it shines with unprecedented light rays of most marvelous activities—
a moonlight of profound twofold benefit
increasing the jubilation of faith for countless beings.

In this garden shaken by the winds formed by clouds of fine explanation,
arises a lotus of fine explanations unheard of before,
from the lake of infinitely vast intelligence,
endowed with the perfect fragrance of the essential meaning.

This having been beautified by clouds of intelligence
and illuminated with garlands of lightning of most amazing confidence,
exalted is this perfect intelligence that roams over the ocean of everything
    there is to know, the entire dimension of the three worlds.

Rongtön, lion of exposition, master of a hundred scriptures,
offered an unprecedented feast of ambrosia of fine explanation,
an ornament adorning the speech of many scholars.

By the excellent abundance of virtues of all kinds derived thereby,
and the vast space-like merit obtained by this work,
may all beings dwelling in this ocean of existence
cross over to the farthest shore,
and acquire the splendor and might of jewel-like omniscience.

This completes the *Adornment to Maitreya's Intent,* a commentary on the treatise entitled *Madhyāntavibhāga, Distinguishing the Middle from the Extremes.*

APPENDIX 1: ILLUMINATING THE ESSENCE

Stages of Meditation Based on the Madhyāntavibhāga,
Distinguishing the Middle from the Extremes

Homage to the guru and the supreme deity.

Dharmakāya realized, you display a mandala of form bodies,
the light of whose enlightened deeds dispels the darkness of the three worlds,
compassionately taking care of us all.
I bow my head to the lotus feet of Śākyamuni, the supreme sage.

Looking after us all with a loving heart,
you offer a feast of sacred Dharma to limitless beings.
To Maitreya, the Dharma regent residing in Tuṣita,
protector of beings, I pay homage.

Showing us the excellent path of liberation,
Maitreya's excellent words are like the sun,
illuminating the vast range of fields of knowledge.
I shall lay out the pith instructions on his *Middle and Extremes*.

The three natures are explained first, because it is necessary to penetrate their meaning before engaging in the practice of the path that will allow one to obtain liberation and the state of omniscience. The three natures are the imputed, the dependent, and the perfected.

The imputed is to be understood as nonexistent in actuality. The dependent is the conceptual thinking that apprehends the objects of perception as truly existent. This conceptual thinking is what needs to be abandoned. The perfected is explained as having two aspects. The first is the object aspect, which is emptiness, empty of the imputed. This is the unchanging perfected. The second aspect is the subject that directly realizes this, gnosis or pristine awareness. This is the unmistaken perfected.

How do we make this our path?

Liberation and omniscience are obtained by realizing the perfected. For that, the stains that obscure one from seeing it must be cleared away. This is why we are taught to identify the obscuring stains. They consist of the veil of afflictions and the cognitive veil.

> Both veils are exhausted here.[1]
> It is held that liberation is attained upon their exhaustion. (2.17)

To relinquish the two veils, one must realize reality. This is why the nature of reality and its ten divisions are taught. To relinquish the veils, one must cultivate the antidote, which is the realization of suchness. Therefore the antidote is taught. To cultivate the antidote, one must understand the process of cultivation. For this purpose the yoga of cultivation is taught. The yoga of cultivation, the antidote, consists of the thirty-seven factors of awakening.

Also, since one needs to cultivate the antidote in terms of both calm abiding and superior insight, these are explained next. Calm abiding is taught in the following terms:

> [. . .] the eight formative factors that eliminate the five faults. (4.3d)

The five faults are taught as follows:

> Laziness, forgetting the instructions,
> sinking and agitation,
> not applying, and applying:
> these are held to be the five faults. (4.4)

The antidotes are the eight formative factors taught in the following stanza:

> The basis and that which is based on it,
> cause and result,
> Not forgetting the point of reference,
> noticing sinking and agitation,
> applying antidotes in order to abandon them,
> and, once they are pacified, to abide in the genuine state of
>   samadhi. (4.5)

[From the thirty-seven factors of awakening,] the five faculties and the five powers, and so forth, are taught as the method to accomplish special insight. These are the dharmas common to all vehicles.

The dharmas of the unsurpassed vehicle are the ten pāramitās and the ten Dharma activities, which are:

Writing, venerating, offering, etc. [...] (5.9a)

The branch of knowledge acquired for the benefit of others consists of ten fields of expertise to be trained in. What are those ten? They are the skandhas, the elements of perception (dhātus), the sources of perception (āyatanas), the four truths, dependent arising, that which definitely occurs and that which cannot, the faculties, time, the vehicles, the compounded, and the uncompounded.

The result that is to be attained is the dharmakāya, accomplished as a result of gradually traversing the ten grounds by means of the ten pāramitās.

In brief, by knowing the three natures, reality is deeply understood. Through the cultivation of the yoga of the thirty-seven factors of awakening, the two veils are relinquished and liberation is gained. Journeying with the unsurpassed vehicle, one engages in ten pāramitās, ten Dharma activities, and ten fields of expertise.

The stages of engaging in the unsurpassed vehicle, taught in brief in the last two stanzas, are explained in the following way:

Based on one's spiritual disposition, one generates conviction in the great vehicle. Then, understanding bodhicitta to be the root of the Mahayana, one generates this mind, which is the resolve to attain supreme awakening. To fully accomplish this resolve, one must perfectly practice the six pāramitās. Further, one initially generates the wisdom realizing the ultimate, and then strives to enhance [one's realization]. One who, over time, practices properly in this way, will eventually proceed to nonconceptual gnosis and nonabiding nirvana. Then, having actualized the dharmakāya, an uninterrupted stream of enlightened activities will emerge.

A vast range of fields of knowledge perfectly explained and understood, abide by its study, contemplation, and meditation to remove the two veils, then expound its meaning to others as the means to attain liberation. These are the unsurpassed vehicle's special characteristics, whose stages of practice are well presented here.

Whatever goodness I have obtained by offering these instructions,
I dedicate to all beings of the three times, my parents.
May it become the cause for their unsurpassed awakening.

May we perfectly realize this profound Dharma,
never parting from its study and contemplation,
and actualize its real essential meaning,
free of exaggeration and denial.

These pith instructions on Distinguishing the Middle from the Extremes *were composed by Rongtön Chenpo at the monastery of Nalendra.*

Appendix 2: Detailed Outline of the Commentary

1. Opening Verses of Worship and Explanation of the Narrative
2. Explanation of the Title
   2.1. Translation of the title
   2.2. Explanation of the title
3. Explanation of the Treatise
   3.1. Presentation of the main body of the treatise
   3.2. Extensive explanation of the branches
      3.2.1. Explanation of the first chapter: Characteristics
         3.2.1.1. The characteristics of total affliction
            3.2.1.1.1. The characteristics in terms of existence and nonexistence (1.1–2)
            3.2.1.1.2. Particular characteristics (1.3–4)
            3.2.1.1.3. The characteristics of total affliction in terms of what it comprises (1.5)
            3.2.1.1.4. The characteristics of total affliction in terms of a means (1.6–7)
            3.2.1.1.5. The characteristics of total affliction in terms of its subdivisions (1.8ab)
            3.2.1.1.6. The characteristics of total affliction in terms of its categories (1.8cd)
            3.2.1.1.7. The characteristics of total affliction in terms of its function (1.9)
            3.2.1.1.8. The characteristics of total affliction (1.10–11)
         3.2.1.2. The characteristics of complete purification
            3.2.1.2.1. Brief summary (1.12)
            3.2.1.2.2. Detailed explanation
               3.2.1.2.2.1. The characteristics of emptiness (1.13)
               3.2.1.2.2.2. The synonyms (1.14–15)
               3.2.1.2.2.3. The divisions of emptiness

3.2.3.2.3. Unmistaken reality (3.5c–3.8a)

3.2.3.2.4. Reality in terms of result and cause

    3.2.3.2.4.1. The truth of suffering presented in terms of fundamental reality (3.8b)

    3.2.3.2.4.2. The truth of origination presented in terms of the three aspects of reality (3.8cd)

    3.2.3.2.4.3. The truth of cessation presented in terms of fundamental reality (3.9ab)

    3.2.3.2.4.4. The truth of the path presented in terms of fundamental reality (3.9c–3.10a)

3.2.3.2.5. Coarse and subtle reality

    3.2.3.2.5.1. The coarse: divisions of the conventional (3.10bc)

    3.2.3.2.5.2. The subtle: divisions of the ultimate (3.10d–3.11)

3.2.3.2.6. Reality as it is generally known (3.12ab)

3.2.3.2.7. Reality in terms of the domain of purity (3.12cd)

3.2.3.2.8. Containing reality (3.13)

3.2.3.2.9. Reality in terms of its differentiated characteristics (3.14)

3.2.3.2.10. Reality in terms of expertise

    3.2.3.2.10.1. Explanation of the belief in a self (3.15–16ab)

    3.2.3.2.10.2. Expressing the antidotes in terms of the three natures (3.16cd)

    3.2.3.2.10.3. Explanation of expertise in the antidotes

        3.2.3.2.10.3.1. The meaning of the skandhas (3.17ab)

        3.2.3.2.10.3.2. Explanation of the elements of perception (3.17cd)

        3.2.3.2.10.3.3. Explanation of the sources of perception (3.18ab)

        3.2.3.2.10.3.4. Explanation of dependent arising (3.18cd)

        3.2.3.2.10.3.5. Explanation of that which definitely occurs and that which cannot (3.19)

        3.2.3.2.10.3.6. Explanation of the twenty-two faculties (3.20ab)

        3.2.3.2.10.3.7. Explanation of time (3.20cd)

        3.2.3.2.10.3.8. Explanation of the truths (3.21)

NOTES

TRANSLATOR'S INTRODUCTION

1. *Cūla-Mālunkyovada Sutta: The Shorter Instructions to Malunkya*, Majjhima Nikāya 63.

2. One system prevalent in the Pāli tradition is that of the eightfold ārya path, in which the first element is right view (*saṃyagdṛṣṭi; yang dag pa'i lta ba*). In the Tibetan tradition, view is referred to in the often-cited triad of view, meditation, and conduct (*lta sgom spyod*).

3. Usually referred to as the *four noble truths*, i.e., the truths of suffering, its origin, its cessation, and the path leading to its cessation. Ārya in this context means "noble one" and refers to those exalted beings who have successfully entered the path and achieved the various levels of awakening. The four truths taught by the Buddha are a reality for these beings and are therefore called "truths of the āryas" or ārya truths.

4. Some scholars distinguish three Mahayana schools of thought: Middle Way (*madhyamaka; dbu ma*), Mind Only (*cittamātra; sems tsam*), and Buddha Nature (*tathāgatagarbha; de gshegs snying po*).

5. The authors of the works listed here are given according to traditional Tibetan scholarship, which is sometimes at odds with the Chinese tradition in this regard.

6. Karl Brunnhölzl, *Center of the Sunlit Sky* (Ithaca: Snow Lion Publication, 2004), 458.

7. This particular statement is found in the *Daśabhūmika* as quoted in Candrakīrti's autocommentary on the *Madhyamakāvatāra*. See La Vallée Poussin 1970, 181, 183.

8. For more details see Mario D'Amato, *Maitreya's Distinguishing the Middle from the Extremes (Madhyāntavibhāga), along with Vasubandhu's Commentary (Madhyāntavibhāga-bhāṣya): A Study and Annotated Translation* (New York: American Institute of Buddhist Studies, 2012), 13–14.

9. See Lambert Schmithausen, On the Problem of the Relation of Spiritual Practice and Philosophical Theory in Buddhism," in *German Scholars on India. Contributions to Indian Studies*, vol. II (New Dehli: Nachiketa Publications Ltd., 1976) 235–50.

10. Ibid., 240f.

11. A great deal of academic research has been carried out on the ālaya consciousness. For detailed presentations, refer for instance to: Lambert Schmithausen,

"Ālayavijñāna: On the Origin and Early Development of a Central Concept of Yogācāra Philosóphy," *Studia Philologica Buddhica Monograph Series*, vol. IV ab (Tokyo: International Institute for Buddhist Studies, 1987); or William Waldron, *The Buddhist Unconscious. The Alayavijñāna in the Context of Indian Buddhist Thought* (New York: Routledge, 2003). For a detailed discussion of the ālaya by a Sakya scholar, see Bsod nams seng ge, "*phung khams skye mched kyi rnam gzhag ji snyed shes bya'i sgo 'byed,*" in gsung 'bum/_bsod nams seng+ge. TBRC W11249, vol. 4 (Dehradun: Sakya College, 1979), 359–476.

12. In Theravāda, this question is answered with the concept of *bhavaṅga-citta*, "a function of consciousness by which the continuity of the individual is preserved through the duration of any single existence, from conception to death." See Bikkhu Bodhi, *A Comprehensive Manual of Abhidhamma*, 106f. In certain respects, the idea of *bhavaṅga* comes quite close to that of the *ālaya*. One major difference, however, is that the *bhavaṅga* is suspended or arrested when the mind engages in an active process of perception, while the *ālaya* is said to flow continuously even when other mental processes are active.

13. D'Amato references Alan Sponberg's article, "The Trisvabhāva Doctrine in India and China," in *Ryūkoku Daigaku Bukkyō Bunka Kenkyūjo Kiyō* vol. 22 (1983): 97–119. See D'Amato, Distinguishing the Middle from the Extremes, 15ff.

14. For a detailed analysis of the status of Yogācāra in Tibet, see Dorji Wangchuk, "On the Status of the Yogācāra School in Tibetan Buddhism," in *The Foundation for Yoga Practitioners: The Buddhist Yogācārabhūmi Treatise and Its Adaptation in India, East Asia, and Tibet*, ed. Ulrich Timme Kragh (Cambridge: Harvard Oriental Series 75, Department of South Asian Studies, 2013), 1316–28.

15. See Jamgon Ju Mipham, *Speech of Delight: Mipham's Commentary of Shantarakshita's Ornament of the Middle Way*, trans. Thomas H. Doctor (Ithaca: Snow Lion Publications, 2004) and Padmakara Translation Group, trans., *The Adornment of the Middle Way: Shantarakshita's Madhyamakalankara with Commentary by Jamgön Mipham* (Boston: Shambhala Publications, 2005).

16. For an overview of the Indian origins of Zhentong Madhyamaka and its early history in Tibet, see Karl Brunnhölzl, *Prajñāpāramitā, Indian "gzhan stong pas," and the Beginning of Tibetan gzhan ston* (Vienna: Arbeitskreis Fur Tibetische und Buddhistische Studien Universität Wien, 2011), and also Brunnhölzl, *The Center of the Sunlit Sky*, 455ff.

17. See Brunnhölzl, *The Center of the Sunlit Sky*, 500ff. and Cyrus Stearns, *The Buddha from Dölpo. A Study of the Life and Thought of the Tibetan Master Dölpopa sherab Gyaltsen* (Ithaca: Snow Lion Publications, 2010).

18. For instance, according to Shakya Chokden, Madhyamaka and Cittamātra are identical in that they both refute the existence of external phenomena. With regard to the way they establish the nonexistence of the apprehending

mind, both the Alīkākāra (usually regarded as a subschool of the Cittamātra, which Shakchok called "Great Madhyamaka") and the Niḥsvabhāvavāda (of the Madhyamaka) are equally profound. See Yaroslav Komarovski, "Echoes of Empty Luminosity: Reevaluation and Unique Interpretation of Yogācāra and Niḥsvabhāvavāda Madhyamaka by the Fifteenth-Century Tibetan Thinker Śākya mchog ldan" (PhD thesis, UVA, 2007).

19. See Padmakara, *Adornment of the Middle Way*, 26–27.

20. As some authors have pointed out, this discrepancy might stem from the fact that both views are held to be provisional from the perspective of Dzogchen (*rdzogs chen*), which is Mipham's ultimate view. See Karma Phuntsho, *Mipham's Dialectics and the Debates on Emptiness: To Be, Not To Be, or Neither* (London: Routledge, 2005), 16ff.

21. Wangchuk, "On the Status of the Yogācāra School," 1323 distinguishes three approaches to Yogācāra in Tibet: negativistic—basically refuting its validity; positivistic—reinterpreting Cittāmatrin notions in light of either the tathāgatagarbha theory or the Great Madhyamaka; and inclusivistic—where Yogācāra represents an independent means that can be combined with Madhyamaka to reach the supreme view.

22. According to the Chinese tradition, the *Treatise on the Sublime Continuum* is attributed not to Maitreya but to Sāramati, an Indian master who flourished around 250 C.E.

23. The root text along with its two Indian commentaries is found in the *sems tsam* section of the Tengyur (Toh. 4021, 4027, and 4032). It has been translated several times into English based on Sanskrit, most recently by D'Amato (2012), which includes Vasubandhu's commentary. Sthiramati's commentary has been translated with the root text and Vasubandhu's commentary by Richard Stanley, "A Study of the *Madhyāntavibhāga-Bhaṣya-Ṭīkā*" (PhD thesis, Australian National University, 1988).

24. See Klaus-Dieter Mathes, "Unterscheidung der Gegebenheiten von ihrem wahren Wesen (Dharmadharmatāvibhāga)" in *Indica et Tibetica* 26 (Swisttal-Odendorf: Indica et Tibetica Verlag,1996), 11–17.

25. As a "nonaffirming negation," emptiness merely negates the existence of something (inherent existence) without affirming the existence of something else instead by implication.

26. This section, extracted from Christian Bernert, "Rong-ston on Buddha-Nature: A Commentary on the Fourth Chapter of the Ratnagotravibhāga" (master's thesis, University of Vienna, 2009), is mainly based on David P. Jackson, *Rong-ston on the Prajñāpāramitā Philosophy of the Abhisamayālaṃkāra: His Subcommentary on Haribhadra's "Sphuṭārthā"* (Kyoto: Nagata Bunshōdō,1988) and Chogay Trichen, *The History of the Sakya Tradition: A Feast for the Minds of the Fortunate*, (Bristol: Ganesha Press,1983).

27. For the list of these teachers given by Shakya Chokden, see Jackson, *Rong-ston on the Prajñāpāramitā Philosophy of the Abhisamayālaṃkāra*, ii–iv.

28. For a detailed explanation of this title see David P. Jackson, "Rong ston bKa' bcu pa. Notes on the title and travels of a great Tibetan scholastic" in *Pramāṇakīrtiḥ: Papers dedicated to Ernst Steinkellner on the occasion of his 70th birthday*, vol. 1, ed. by Birgit Kellner, et al. (Vienna: Arbeitskreis für Tibetische und Buddhistische Studien, Universität Wien, 2007), 345–60.

29. Jackson gives the following tentative list of ten treatises based on Rongtön's own studies and personal interests: (1) *Abhisamayālaṃkāra;* (2) *Pramāṇaviniścaya;* (3) *Abhidharmasamuccaya;* (4) *Abhidharmakośa;* (5) *Vinaya;* (6) *Ratnagotravibhāga;* (7–9) possibly the *Mahāyānasūtrālaṃkāra, Dharmadharmatāvibhāga* and *Madhyāntavibhāga;* and (10) either a Madhyamaka treatise or another Pramāṇa scripture. Jackson, "Rong ston bKa' bcu pa," 350.

30. Jackson gives a list of twenty-one treatises that Rongtön taught during his career, on which he did not compose commentaries. Jackson, *Rong-ston on the Prajñāpāramitā Philosophy of the Abhisamayālaṃkāra*, v.

31. Ibid., iv.

32. Such as Nyame Sherab Gyaltsen (1356–1415), who studied Buddhist philosophy under Rongtön.

33. See the list given by Shakya Chokden in ibid., vi–viii.

34. Jackson, *Early Abbots of 'Phan-po Nalendra*, 6.

35. Jackson, *Rong-ston on the Prajñāpāramitā Philosophy of the Abhisamayālaṃkāra*, v.

36. On Rongtön's critique of Tsongkhapa see Mamoru Kobayashi, "The Madhyamaka Thought of Roṅ ston Śākya rgyal mtshan and Its Impact" in *Memoirs of the Research Department of the Toyo Bunko No. 63* (Tokyo: The Toyo Bunko, 2005), 15–23.

37. See Jackson, "Rong ston bKa' bcu pa," 352–56.

38. Jackson, *Rong-ston on the Prajñāpāramitā Philosophy of the Abhisamayālaṃkāra*, xiv. See also Chogay Trichen, *History of the Sakya Tradition*, 30.

39. Ibid., x–xi; and Jackson, *Early Abbots of 'Phan-po Nalendra*, 7–8.

40. In the fourteenth century, the Phamo Drupa clan took control of Tibet from the Sakyapas, and this lasted until internal instability led to their collapse in 1434.

41. This master, who served as the last abbot of this monastery before the cultural revolution, was recognized as the eighteenth incarnation in the line of Khyenrab Chöje (1436–1497), the eighth abbot of Nālendra.

42. Chogay Trichen Rinpoche, *History of the Sakya Tradition*, 31.

43. Jackson, Early Abbots of 'Phan-po Nalendra, 63.

44. For this section we consulted Khentsun Sangpo (1979): *Biographical Dictionary of Tibet and Tibetan Buddhism*, vol. 11. Dharamsala: Library of Tibetan Works and Archives; and Chogay Trichen, *History of the Sakya Tradition*.

45. Kamalaśīla was a master of the Svātantrika Madhyamaka philosophy and author of the *Madhyamakāloka (Dbu ma snang ba*, Derge no. 3887), which

Rongtön studied at Sangphu. Haribhādra was (like Rongtön) an important commentator on the *Abhisamayālaṃkāra*.

46. A tantric practice introduced to Tibet by the master Phadampa Sangye (fl. eleventh century C.E.).

47. The six are: Rongtön's teacher, Yaktön Sangye Pel (1350–1414), and Rongtön Mawe Senge (1367–1449), known for their mastery of the sūtra teachings; Ngorchen Kunga Sangpo (1382–1456) and Dzongpa Kunga Namgyal (1432–1496), known for their expertise in the tantras; and Rongtön's students, Gorampa Sönam Senge (1428–1489) and Shakya Chokden (1428–1507), masters in both the sūtras and the tantras. See Chogay Trichen, *History of the Sakya Tradition*, 27.

48. Sachen Kunga Nyingpo (1092–1158), Lopön Sönam Tsemo (1142–1182), Jetsün Dragpa Gyaltsen (1147–1216), Sakya Pandita Kunga Gyaltsen (1182–1251), and Drogön Chögyal Phagpa (1235–1280).

49. For a translation of these two commentaries see Dharmachakra Translation Committee, *Middle Beyond Extremes: Maitreya's Madhyantavibhaga with Commentaries by Khenpo Shenga and Ju Mipham* (Ithaca: Snow Lion Publications, 2006).

50. This is of course related to the teachers responsible for establishing Buddhism in Tibet and their local supporters. In Japan and China, for instance, the transmission of the Yogācāra tradition played a much greater role.

51. Gadjin M. Nagao, ed., *Madhyantavibhaga-bhasya: A Buddhist Philosophical Treatise Edited for the First Time from a Sanskrit Manuscript* (Tokyo: Suzuki Research Foundation, 1964).

52. www.tbrc.org.

53. Rong ston rma ba'i seng ge (1998): *dbus mtha' rnam 'byed dang chos dang chos nyid rnam 'byed rtsa 'grel*, Khreng tu'u (Chengdu): Si khron mi rigs dpe skrun khang. This book in Western format includes a biography of Maitreya, the root verses of both the *Madhyāntavibhāga* and the *Dharmadharmatāvibhāga*, along with Rongtön's commentaries and their outlines.

54. For instance, when the responder in a debate wants to emphasize the subject of his proposition, he will mark it by saying "the subject" (chos can) at the end of his utterance. In his writing, Rongtön uses this dialectic tool to call the reader's attention to the subject of debate, engaging him or her directly as if witnessing a live debate (not dissimilar to the use of direct speech in a novel).

CHAPTER 1. OPENING VERSES OF WORSHIP AND EXPLANATION OF THE NARRATIVE

1. kumuda: A type of night-blooming water lily.

2. The first stanza is an homage to Acalā, a wrathful form of Mañjuśrī, and Rongtön's yidam, or personal deity, one of whose names is Mind Treasury (Tib. *blo gter*).

3. Ajita, the "Invincible," is an epithet of Maitreya.

4. This refers to a previous incarnation of the Bodhisattva Maitreya, not to be confused with the Yogācāra master Sthiramati, who composed a commentary on this very text.

CHAPTER 3. EXPLANATION OF THE TREATISE

1. Phrases including the words "the subject" in this way stem from the debate language used in this context. Whatever is written before the words "the subject" in any given clause of this type is the subject of debate, in this case "that which is beyond the two extremes of existence and nonexistence." This kind of language is still used today in the dialectic training in Tibetan philosophical institutions and it is also used in texts, both classical and modern, on Buddhist philosophy and practice. Even though this phrasing is not generally used in English, we decided to retain this wording to give the reader an idea of the debate mode evoked in this text.

2. 'phags pa 'od srung gi le'u zhes bya ba theg pa chen po'i mdo (H 87), 229b2–3.

3. As in the example of the dream, where things appear as real to the dreaming mind, yet do not have any true existence.

4. In other words, certain appearances are labeled "sentient beings" based on the existence of their sense faculties, as opposed to inanimate objects, which do not have sense faculties.

5. According to the oral tradition in the lineage of the Sakya master Khenchen Appey Rinpoche, the aspect of the apprehender is included here as well. It is not in the editions of Rongtön's text, however.

6. "Mind and mental factors without taints" (zag pa med pa) means "free of afflictions."

7. In this context, object is taken in its broadest sense to denote any object of the mind.

8. This means that the mind (visual consciousness in the example above) perceives the nature of the object in a general sense (here a visual object). The mental factors accompanying this consciousness apprehend its particular features, enabling the mind to distinguish this object from everything else.

9. In other words, mind and mental factors are not two separate entities apprehending different objects. They are of one nature and are distinguished on the basis of their specific mode of apprehension of the different aspects of the object.

10. This text is probably by Rongtön himself, but could not be located. Many of his works are unfortunately no longer extant.

11. The other aspect is discussed in the next section.

12. "Becoming" refers to karma in this context.

13. This means that the first three are affliction, the next two karma, and the remaining seven the resultant aspect of birth in a samsaric existence.

14. Tib. tshu rol mthong ba, lit., "those who see this side."

15. In other words, emptiness of the apprehended and apprehender cannot be said to be identical with imagination, because even though they experience imagination, ordinary beings do not realize emptiness.

16. In Yogācāra philosophy one of the primary meanings of the term dhātu is "cause." See Nobuyoshi Yamabe, "Riposte," in *Pruning the Bodhi Tree: The Storm Over Critical Buddhism,* Paul Loren Swanson and Jamie Hubbard, eds. (Honolulu: University of Hawai'i Press, 1997), 208–19.

17. The veil of afflictions and the cognitive veil.

18. The veil of afflictions.

19. Śrāvaka-, pratyekabuddha-, and bodhisattvagotras.

20. These are the afflictions that are not rooted in a particular philosophical view or understanding. They are desire, anger, ignorance, pride, and doubt.

21. These are distorted views of reality. They are (1) the view of the perishing collection (*'jig lta*), which is the belief in the existence of a permanent identity based on a collection of perishing phenomena (the five skandhas); (2) extreme views (*mthar lta*), the belief in permanence and annihilation; and (3) wrong views (*log lta*), beliefs that totally oppose the view of reality taught by the Buddha.

22. *Regarding discipline and ascetic practices as supreme* refers to a specific kind of wrong view, where one believes that rites and austerities that do not bring about liberating insight are a path to liberation.

23. The four wrong views are: clinging to the impure as pure, to the impermanent as permanent, to suffering as happiness, and to that which is devoid of self as the self.

24. *Wrong views* are beliefs which do not accord with reality, such as denying the law of cause and effect.

25. Each of the ten qualities is obstructed by three veils, making thirty veils. Veils 1a, 1b, and 1c obstruct the first quality. Veils 2a, 2b, and 2c obstruct the second, and so forth.

26. According to Sthiramati's commentary, this refers to applying practices that will not be effective in eradicating the afflictions active in oneself. An example given in this context is that of someone afflicted by desire who cultivates loving-kindness, a remedy used to counter anger, not desire. See Stanley, "A Study of the *Madhyāntavibhāga-Bhaṣya-Ṭīkā,*" 99.

27. Here, afflictions and karma function as the cause, the maturation of which is rebirth in samsara.

28. This probably refers to the dormant latencies of these three left in the mind.

29. Such as the ten unwholesome deeds.

30. Referring to the Mahayana teachings.

31. The path of cultivation abandons greater, middling, and lesser cognitive veils, each again being subdivided into greater, middling, and lesser aspects (great-great, middle-great, lesser-great; great-middle, middle-middle, small-middle; great-small, middle-small, small-small). The remaining veils are the subtlest veils to be purified on the path of cultivation.

32. See glossary.

33. According to Vasubandhu's *Abhidharmakośa,* the productive cause (*karaṇa-hetu; byed rgyu*) is one of the six types of causes (*hetu; rgyu*) and four conditions (*pratyaya; rkyen*) active in the production of compounded phenomena. See Louis de La Vallée Poussin, *Abhidharmakośabhāṣyam,* vol. 1, Leo M. Pruden, trans. (Berkeley: Asian Humanities Press, 1991), 255ff.

34. The text reads "ten veils" (*sgrib pa bcu*), which, according to the commentary, must be a corrupt reading.

35. These are the sustenance of material food (*kham*), of touch (*reg pa*), of volition (*sems pa*), and of consciousness (*rnam shes*).

36. These two stanzas, originally from Vasubandhu's commentary, the *Madhyāntavibhāga-bhāṣya,* are included in the Derge edition of the root text, but not in the Peking edition.

37. "Path of cultivation free from the remaining veils" is a technical term. Here, "remaining veils" probably refers to a portion of the veils abandoned on the path of seeing (*mthong spangs*). It is also true that it is the path of cultivation that removes the cognitive veils, which remain after one has accomplished the path of seeing.

38. This refers to the practice of dedication of the bodhisattvas on the grounds.

39. In other words, not practicing, wrong practices, and practices that are correct but at the time inappropriate.

40. The *individual* in this context refers to a teacher who explains the profound scriptures.

41. These are the thirty-seven factors conducive to awakening (*bodhipakṣya-dharma; byang chub phyogs mthun kyi chos*): the four close applications of mindfulness (*smṛtyupasthāna; dran pa nyer gzhag*), the four perfect abandonments (*samyak-pradhāna; yang dag spong ba*), the four causes of miraculous power (*ṛddhipāda; rdzu 'phrul gyi rkang pa*), the five faculties (*indriya; dbang po*), the five powers (*bala; stobs*), the seven limbs of awakening (*bodhyaṅga; byang chub kyi yan lag*), and the eightfold ārya path (*āryāṣṭāṅgika-mārga; 'phags lam yang lag brgyad*).

42. The close application of mindfulness is applied to the body, feelings, the mind, and phenomena.

43. The four perfect abandonments are the abandonment of unwholesome factors that have already arisen, the prevention of unwholesome factors that have not been generated from arising, the generation of wholesome factors that have not yet arisen, and the increasing of the wholesome factors that have been generated.

44. The four are causes of miraculous power are intention (*vīrya; 'dun pa*), will (*vicāra; sems*), diligent perseverance (*chanda; brtson 'grus*), and analysis (*citta; dpyod pa*).

45. The five faculties are faith (*śraddhā; dad pa*), diligent perseverance (*vīrya; brtson 'grus*), mindfulness (*smṛti; dran pa*), samadhi (*samādhi; ting nge 'dzin*), and wisdom (*prajñā; shes rab*).

46. This refers to the wholesome qualities gained on the path of accumulation, which is the first path leading to liberation. The wholesome qualities of the path of joining, which bring about the path of seeing, are called the roots of wholesomeness conducive to definite distinction (*nges 'byed cha mthun*).

47. The five powers refer to the five faculties when they are developed to a higher degree.

48. This refers to the veil of afflictions.

49. This refers to the part of the negativities abandoned through the path of cultivation.

50. The logical consequence implied here is that without affluence one cannot practice giving.

51. *Post-attainment* refers to the wisdom brought about through the power of realization attained in meditative equipoise.

52. "Signs" here refers to any characteristic the conceptual mind clings to and that is attributed to an object of perception. In the case of bodhisattvas, this clinging does not entail clinging to any true existence of the objects, but merely to their signs, such as "male," "female," "long," "short," and so forth.

53. The four perfect discriminations are four aspects of a bodhisattva's correct understanding of things. They refer to a correct understanding of phenomena (dharmas), of meanings (i.e., various types of phenomena), of words (language), and of confidence (with regard to understanding the Dharma).

54. This spiritual disposition (*gotra; rigs*) refers to the naturally present disposition or the potential for realization present in all beings, as opposed to the developed disposition, which is present only in those who have generated bodhicitta.

55. "Nonafflicted ignorance" indicates that this ignorance refers to the cognitive veil. The veil of afflictions was discarded upon attaining the first ground.

56. The Tibetan in the following passage seems to be corrupt in all editions available to us, as the three definitions of the characteristics of reality in terms of the three natures seem to be identical. We based our reading on Vasubandhu's and Mipham's commentaries.

57. In other words, since the imputed is "never existent," it may be referred to as the opposite of permanent, defined as "always existent."

58. The suffering of suffering, the suffering of change, and the all-pervasive suffering of conditioned existence.

59. Suffering is that which is characterized by a specific property (*chos can*), and the perfected is that very property (*chos nyid*). In other words, the nature of suffering itself is the perfected.

60. Literally, "emptiness in terms of not being the entity that is that nonexistence." This means that because the dependent is asserted to be substantially existent, it is not mere nonexistence.

61. See commentary to 3.6cd.

62. In the case of ordinary beings, the perfected nature is not purified of defilements, and this is the origin of their suffering.

63. As Rongtön states in his *Illuminating the Essence,* the dependent is dualistic thought, which needs to be eliminated. See p. 109.

64. The abstract notion (*don spyi*) of the ultimate is not the actual ultimate but the concept of it formed in one's mind.

65. Literally, the "ultimate ultimate."

66. The first refers to emptiness, the second to the gnosis that realizes emptiness.

67. A third type of general knowledge, i.e., that which is generally known in the treatises (*bstan bcos la grags pa*), is probably included in the second type of knowledge.

68. Of these three, scripture (*āgama; lung*) is accepted as a means of valid cognition if it is not harmed by or does not contradict the other two means, i.e., valid direct perception (*pratyakṣa; mngon sum*) and valid inference (*anumāna; rjes dpag*).

69. According to Sthiramati, these five entities are explained as subsuming all phenomena. See Stanley, "A Study of the *Madhyāntavibhāga-Bhaṣya-Ṭīkā*," 175.

70. This refers to suchness as superior to all other categories mentioned above (i.e., the two other natures), as well as the unmistaken perfected.

71. The sutra explains these seven aspects of reality in the following way (in a different order than in this treatise). (1) The reality of involvement refers to the beginningless and endless nature of samsaric existence; (2) the reality of the characteristics refers to the selflessness of phenomena and of the individual; (3) the reality of cognition stands for the realization that phenomena are nothing but mental representations; (4) the reality of abiding refers to the truth of suffering; (5) the reality of wrong engagement refers to the truth of the origin of suffering; (6) the reality of purification refers to the truth of cessation; and (7) the reality of genuine engagement refers to the truth of the path. For a translation of the relevant passage see Powers (1995), 171–72.

72. According to Sthiramati, beginningless involvement in samsara is contained in the *imputed* because it does not really exist, and in the *dependent* because the beings caught in this illusion have this experience based on causes and conditions.

73. *Abiding* means that the formative factors abide in the nature of suffering.

74. Tib. *gnas dang gnas ma yin.* This refers to the correct understanding of karma, cause, and result.

75. This refers to the belief that it is the self that attains liberation.

76. As seen in the last section (3.15–16ab), expertise in the skandhas is the first of ten antidotes to the belief in a self.

77. According to Sthiramati's explanation, the three types of form refer to the imputed, the dependent, and the perfected, respectively. Stanley, "A Study of the *Madhyāntavibhāga-Bhaṣya-Ṭīkā*," 184.

78. The twelve sources of perception describe the process of perception from the point of view of the causes of the arising of future consciousness, whereas the

eighteen elements of perception explain the same process from the point of view of the continuity of perception based on the already arisen experience.

79. The text reads *yongs su spyod pa'i nyer spyod*. We followed the reading of the root text, which is *yongs su gcod pa'i nyer spyod*.

80. In this context, a creative cause could be a creator god, and a principal entity, a primal natural force like the concept of *prakṛti* in Indian Saṃkhya philosophy.

81. In Indian mythology, a cakravartin universal emperor is a worldly ruler who has control over vast areas of the universe.

82. This is the prevalent view in the Mahayana tradition, the understanding of which requires further explanation. As stated in the introduction, the Buddha's teachings are like medicine adapted to the condition of his disciples. It is therefore important to consider the historical and cultural context in which those discourses were delivered. In ancient India, women definitely did not enjoy the same rights as they do today in developed countries. For a general audience, the teachings had to be culturally adapted in order to attract and gradually train disciples. On a philosophical level, the matter is presented differently. An important Mahayana sūtra, the *Vimalakīrtinirdeśa*, rejects gender-based ideas, claiming that the concepts *male* and *female* do not have any bearing in the light of enlightened wisdom. On the conventional level, however, the common Mahayana maintains that a buddha always manifests in male form. According to the tantric vehicle, on the other hand, buddhahood can be attained by women, just as tantric buddhas appear in female forms.

83. The six faculties of eyes, ears, nose, tongue, body, and mind.

84. Physically pleasant and unpleasant sensations, mental happiness and unhappiness, and neutral sensations.

85. These five faculties are faith, diligent perseverance, mindfulness, meditative absorption, and wisdom. They are included in the thirty-seven factors conducive to awakening, and are features of the path of ordinary beings before the attainment of the path of seeing. This is why they control "worldly purity." The thirty-seven factors are divided into seven groups: the first three (four close applications of mindfulness, four perfect abandonments, and four bases for miraculous activity) are cultivated on the small, middle, and great paths of accumulation respectively; the five faculties are cultivated on the first and second stages of the path of joining and the five powers on its last two stages; the seven limbs of awakening are cultivated on the path of seeing, and the eightfold ārya path on the path of cultivation.

86. These are the three untainted faculties (*zag med dbang po lnga*) of ārya beings on the paths of seeing, of cultivation, and of no further training, respectively.

87. These are the last two categories of purity: the five faculties and the three untainted faculties.

88. The Derge edition of the root text has two lines at this point, omitted in both the Peking and Narthang editions: "Their cause is that which brings about, it

is the truth of origination." We did not include them in our text, as Rongtön does not comment on them.

89. "Definite emergence" renders *nges par 'byung ba,* which is also translated as "renunciation." This term carries the dual meaning of renunciation of samsara and longing for liberation.

90. *Designations* refers to all verbal conventions used to designate phenomena. *Productive causes* designates the seed part of the all-base consciousness.

91. *Suffering of that which is nothing but negativity* refers to the suffering of conditioned existence that pervades all aspects of samsaric existence. As seen above, the negativities are karma, afflictions, and rebirth within samsara.

92. The five supernatural powers are divine sight, divine hearing, knowing the minds of others, recollecting past lives, and the ability to perform miraculous deeds. To this list of five is added one power possessed only by buddhas, the knowledge of the exhaustion of afflictions.

93. *Pliancy* refers to the serviceability of both body and mind, resulting from powerful states of meditative concentration.

94. That is to say, the power of diligent perseverance results from faith, mindfulness from perseverance, samadhi from mindfulness, and wisdom from samadhi.

95. The term *sems bskyed pa* (Skt. *cittotpāda*) is short for *byang chub tu sems bskyed pa* (Skt. *bodhicittotpāda*), which literally translates as "the generation of a mind focused on awakening." Practitioners of each of the three vehicles generate such resolve. They differ in terms of the form of awakening they intend to attain, namely arhathood, pratyekabuddhahood, or the perfect enlightenment of a fully realized buddha.

96. See below for a discussion of the five results (3.2.4.3.1.).

97. Or "arrival."

98. The *ground of convinced conduct* refers to the paths of accumulation and joining, when one has attained a convinced understanding of the ultimate nature through study and contemplation.

99. The *mind that perfectly knows to discriminate* refers to a specific realization is first attained on the ninth ground. It encompasses the perfect understanding of phenomena, of meanings, of words, and of confidence.

100. This does not refer to empowerment according to the Secret Mantra tradition. Here, the buddhas empower the bodhisattvas on the tenth ground as their regents, like Maitreya in Tuṣita.

101. For a description of the five results see Vasubandhu's *Abhidharmakośa.* For a translation see La Vallée Poussin, *Abhidharmakośabhāṣyam,* 286ff. Also refer to David Karma Choephel, *Jewels from the Treasury: Vasubandhu's* Verses on the Treasury of Abhidharma *and Its Commentary* Youthful Play *by the Ninth Karmapa Wangchuk Dorje* (Woodstock: KTD Publications, 2012).

102. The Tibetan term *dmigs pa* (Skt. *ālambana*) covers a broader semantic field than its English equivalents. In this section it refers to both support (or basis) and focal object.

103. The treasury of space is attained on the first bodhisattva ground based on a specific samadhi that carries the same name: the samadhi of the treasury of space. It allows one to perfect the practice of giving by infinitely increasing and multiplying the objects one gives away, by means of meditative concentration.

104. Discussing the meaning of the term *pāramitā*, Donald S. Lopez, in *The Heart Sutra Explained: Indian and Tibetan Commentaries* (Albany: SUNY Press, 1988), 21, explains its dual meaning based on its two etymologies: the "highest" (from the word *parama*) and "that which has gone beyond" (from *pāra* and *mita*). Tibetan translators chose the second reading when rendering the term with the phrase *pha rol tu phyin pa* (*pha rol tu* "to the other side" and *phyin pa* "gone").

105. "Harm" refers to the seven unwholesome deeds of body and speech (i.e., killing, taking what is not given, sexual misconduct, lying, harsh words, divisive talk, and idle speech), and "basis" refers to the three unwholesome deeds of the mind (i.e., covetousness, ill-will, and wrong views).

106. In the context of discussing mind and mental factors, I render the term *yid la byed pa* (Skt. *manaskāra*) as *attention*, which is a common translation. In other contexts, when the term is used in a more general sense, I choose *mental engagement,* as in this passage.

107. Sutras and melodic verses are two of the twelve branches of scripture (*gsung rab kyi yan lag bcu gnyis*). See the glossary for a full list. For further details see Eugene Obermiller, *The Jewelry of Scripture of Bu-ston* (Delhi: Sri Satguru,1987), 31–34.

108. Here, element (*dhātu; khams*) is synonymous with spiritual disposition (*gotra; rigs*).

109. The phrase *tshig kha ton du byed pa* means to recite out loud what has been memorized.

110. The Tibetan term translated as "syllable" is *yi ge*, which means the smallest unit of speech. This term is also translated as "letter," but since letters are visual representations of sounds, this definition is too narrow in this context.

111. In other words, by understanding that syllables and words are mere mental constructs, the bodhisattva ceases clinging to them and attains nonconceptual awareness.

112. In the first sentence of this paragraph, Rongtön seems to emphasize the way things appear (i.e., the conventional level). On this level, both states, impure and pure, arise adventitiously in the sense that they appear at a certain time, dependent on whether the stains are present or purified. The reasoning he gives in the next sentence relates to the adventitious nature of the stains themselves.

113. In the Tibetan root text, the following lines are preceded by one stanza, which Rongtön explains later. Since neither are part of the actual root text (i.e., they all come from Vasubandhu's commentary), we chose to give them in the order presented here.

114. These lines are included in all the commonly available editions of the Tibetan

translation of the root text. As Rongtön points out, however, they are part of Vasubandhu's commentary, which indicates that Rongtön probably had access to another edition of the root text. This is further supported by the fact that Paramārtha's Chinese translation of the text does not include these lines. See D'Amato, *Maitreya's Distinguishing the Middle from the Extremes,* 182n10.

115. In Indian mythology, the vajra, sometimes likened to the thunderbolt, is the indestructible weapon of Indra, the chief deity of the Vedic pantheon.

116. See D'Amato, *Maitreya's Distinguishing the Middle from the Extremes,* 182–83.

117. In the Tibetan root text, this stanza comes before the previous group of lines starting with "Existence and nonexistence [. . .]." See notes 110 and 111.

118. This objection implies that the imputed and the dependent natures are obstructing factors, belonging to conventional reality. If they truly exist, they cannot be natural luminosity, which is the perfected nature, ultimate reality.

119. See notes 113, 114, and 117.

120. The three doors of liberation are emptiness, signlessness, and wishlessness.

121. Here, "basis" translates *dmigs pa* (Skt. *ālambana*). It is used in different ways throughout this passage. In the context of cognition, it is the object used as the focal support for the related consciousness to arise and is therefore rendered as "focal object." In other instances it is used in the general sense of functioning as a basis or support.

122. Here, "worldly path" refers to the path of cultivation during the phase of subsequent attainment, and the "path beyond the world" to the path of cultivation during the phase of meditative equipoise.

123. The eighth ground is called the "Unmoving" because there is no clinging to signs any longer from this stage onward.

124. The four perfect discriminations are four aspects of a bodhisattva's correct understanding of things. They refer to a correct understanding of phenomena (dharmas), of meanings (i.e., the various types of phenomena), of words (language), and of confidence (with regard to his or her understanding of the Dharma).

APPENDIX 1: ILLUMINATING THE ESSENCE

1. This line does not appear in our editions of the root text. The Tibetan reads: *sgrib pa gnyis po der zad de.*

Glossary

afflicted mind (*kliṣṭamanas; nyon mongs pa can gyi yid*).
The afflicted mind is a subtle aspect of consciousness that focuses on the continuum of the all-base consciousness, apprehending it as the self. It is the seventh type of consciousness in the eight-consciousness model of the mind according to Yogācāra.

all-base *or* **all-base consciousness** (*ālayavijñāna; kun gzhi rnam shes*).
The all-base consciousness is the eighth type of consciousness in the eight-consciousness model of the mind according to Yogācāra. It comprises two aspects: the seed part (*sa bon gyi cha*), which is the causal aspect that will produce future results, and the maturation part (*rnam smin gyi cha*), which is the resultant aspect of the produced experience. For a more detailed explanation, see the introduction.

annihilation. See two extremes.

ārya (Skt.); (Tib. *'phags pa*).
Often translated as "noble," it refers to the exalted state of those who have gained direct insight into ultimate reality and thereby have removed the afflictions obstructing liberation.

cognition or representation (*vijñapti; rnam par rig pa*).
The mental cognitions on the basis of which the deluded mind projects the duality of apprehended and apprehender.

complete purification (*vyavadāna; rnam par byang ba*).
All dharmas belonging to nirvāṇa and the path.

dependent nature. See three natures.

dharmadhātu (Skt.); (Tib. *chos dbyings*).
Lit., "dharma expanse." A synonym for emptiness. It is explained in this text as the cause for the properties of an ārya, since by taking it as the focal object of meditation one attains the exalted state.

dharmakāya. See kāya.

dharmatā (Skt.); (Tib. *chos nyid*).
The true nature of things, synonym for ultimate reality and emptiness.

emptiness (*śūnyatā; stong pa nyid*).
In the Yogācāra tradition, emptiness is defined in terms of the three natures as the nonexistence of the imputed nature in the dependent nature, the realization of which is the perfect nature. It is the existence of the nonexistence of the dualistic entities of apprehended objects and the apprehending mind within the imagination of the unreal.

five paths (*pañca-mārga; lam lnga*).
The stages of spiritual progress on the path to awakening. In the Mahayana, the five paths comprise: (1) the path of accumulation (*saṃbhāra-mārga; tshogs lam*), on which the bodhisattva gathers the accumulations of merit and wisdom; (2) the path of joining (*prayoga-mārga; sbyor lam*), where one's practice is mainly focused on the meditation on emptiness; (3) the path of seeing (*darśana-mārga; mthong lam*), which is the direct realization of emptiness; (4) the path of cultivation (*bhāvanā-mārga; sgom lam*), on which one deepens one's realization of emptiness; and (5) the path of no further training (*aśaikṣa-mārga; mi slob lam*), which is the state of complete purity, free of all veils, the state of perfect buddhahood. For details on each path see the corresponding entries in the glossary.

focal object (*ālambana; dmigs pa*).
The object of focus or frame of reference used by consciousness in the dualistic mode of perception.

gnosis (*jñāna; ye shes*).
The knowledge or wisdom exclusive to ārya beings. Also termed "pristine wisdom," "transcendent awareness," and the like.

ground (*bhūmi; sa*).
The ten levels of realization of a bodhisattva, from the initial realization of emptiness to the moment before the attainment of perfect buddhahood. See also path of seeing and path of cultivation.

imagination of the unreal (*abhūta-parikalpa; yang dag pa min pa'i kun tu rtog pa*).
The mind under the influence of a mistaken perception of reality (ignorance), conceiving reality to consist of apprehended objects and the apprehending subject (the mind) as separate entities. Also termed "false imagination," "wrong representation," "conceptual construction of the unreal," and the like.

imputed nature. See three natures.

kāya (Skt.); (Tib. *sku*).

The "bodies" of perfect enlightenment. A buddha's awakening has three levels of manifestation, called the three kāyas. These are (1) the *dharmakāya*, or dharma-body (Tib. *chos sku*), which is a buddha's perfect realization of ultimate reality and is not perceptible by others; (2) the *saṃbhogakāya*, or body of enjoyment (Tib. *longs sku*), which is the pure manifestation of this realization in forms perceptible by bodhisattvas on the highest level of realization; and (3) the *nirmāṇakāya*, or emanation body (Tib. *sprul sku*), which is the manifestation of enlightenment accessible to ordinary beings. Sometimes a fourth kāya is added to this list, the *svabhāvikakāya*, or essence body (Tib. *ngo bo nyid kyi sku*), which refers to the inseparability of the three other kāyas.

latencies (*vāsanā; bag chags*).

The imprints of deeds (of body, speech, and mind) left on the all-base consciousness. Like seeds, latencies have the potential to produce specific results in accordance with their individual nature, but lie inactive until the causes and conditions for them to ripen are met. They then manifest in the form of the various objects of the six senses (pleasant, unpleasant, or neutral in accordance with the nature of the deeds they originate from), which in turn produces the impulse to act and thus produce new latencies. In this way, the vicious circle of samsara is kept alive, until the production of latencies is stopped by realizing that these objects are nothing but mental projections and therefore not real. Also called "habitual tendencies," "karmic propensities," "dispositions," and the like.

nirmāṇakāya. See kāya.

pāramitā (Skt.); (Tib. *pha rol tu phyin pa*).

The qualities cultivated on the path to bring one's spiritual potential to full maturation. The primary six are giving (*dāna; sbyin pa*), ethical discipline (*śīla; tshul khrims*), forbearance (*kṣānti; bzod pa*), diligent perseverance (*vīrya; brtson 'grus*), meditative stability (*dhyāna; bsam gtan*), and wisdom (*prajñā; shes rab*). To this list four more pāramitās are added to complete the bodhisattva path: means (*upāya; thabs*), aspiration (*praṇidhāna; smon lam*), power (*bala; stobs*), and gnosis (*jñāna; ye shes*).

particular characteristics (*svalakṣaṇa; rang gi mtshan nyid*).

The particular features of any given object that distinguish it from all other objects.

path of accumulation (*saṃbhāra-mārga; tshogs lam*).

The first of the five stages of the path to awakening, attained upon generating bodhicitta out of great compassion for sentient beings. The practice on this stage consists of gathering the accumulations of merit by means of altruistically motivated deeds, and of wisdom, mainly based on study and contemplation. The path of accumulation comprises three levels (small, middle, and great), on which one cultivates the four close applications of mindfulness, the four perfect abandonments, and the four causes for miraculous activity respectively.

path of cultivation (*bhāvanā-mārga; sgom lam*).
The fourth of the five stages of the path to awakening. After one has seen emptiness directly for the first time on the previous stage, the path consists of deepening one's realization by cultivating in meditation one's newly gained insight and of the application of the eightfold ārya path. In this way, one gradually removes the cognitive veils, thereby attaining increasingly higher levels of realization (i.e., the second to the tenth bodhisattva grounds).

path of joining (*prayoga-mārga; sbyor lam*).
The second of the five stages of the path to awakening. On this stage one mainly engages in meditation on emptiness, based on the understanding gained on the previous stage. This path is divided into four levels, which represent increasingly higher levels of realization: heat (one starts to feel the "heat" of the "fire of emptiness," which burns away all afflictions), peak (the realization reaches a new summit, on which the roots of wholesomeness become indestructible), forbearance (one is able to fearlessly forbear the reality of emptiness), and supreme dharma (the last phase of worldly existence, immediately preceding the direct realization of emptiness). On the first two of these levels, the bodhisattva cultivates the five faculties, and on the last two, the five powers. This path is called the path of joining because it functions as a link, bringing the mind to the realization of emptiness.

path of no further training (*aśaikṣa-mārga; mi slob lam*).
The fifth and last of the five stages of the path to awakening. Having completely removed both veils, one attains the stage of buddhahood, consisting of the three kāyas of perfect awakening.

path of seeing (*darśana-mārga; mthong lam*).
The third of the five stages of the path to awakening. This path consists of the direct, nonconceptual realization of emptiness, and the accomplishment of the seven limbs of awakening. On this stage, the veil of afflictions is removed and one reaches the first bodhisattva ground (*bhūmi; sa*), thus becoming an ārya being.

perfected nature. See three natures.

permanence. See two extremes.

reality (*tattva; de kho na nyid*).
A synonym for ultimate reality.

samadhi (*samādhi; ting nge 'dzin*).
Meditative concentration or absorption, uninterrupted by the process of discursive thought. The training in samadhi forms one of the three pillars of the Buddhist path; the other two are the trainings in ethical discipline (*śīla; tshul khrims*) and in wisdom (*prajñā; shes rab*).

saṃbhogakāya. See kāya.

sign (*nimitta; mtshan ma*).
The marks or distinguishing characteristics of an object of perception. They are the basic data of perception related to the six senses—including visual forms, sounds, smells, tastes, textures, and concepts—the processing of which enables the conceptual mind to distinguish any given object from all others.

six types of consciousness (*tshogs drug gyi rnam shes*).
The six consciousnesses related to the six sense faculties of the eyes, ears, nose, tongue, touch, and mind.

skandha (Skt.); (Tib. *phung po*).
This term is translated as "aggregate," "heap," or "bundle." The five skandhas are the five groups of psychophysical functional phenomena, making up the entirety of human experience. The five are form (*rūpa; gzugs*), feeling (*vedanā; tshor ba*), discrimination (*saṃjñā; 'du shes*), formative factors (*saṃskāra; 'du byed*), and consciousness (*vijñāna; rnam shes*). The self of the individual is imputed on the basis of these five skandhas.

spiritual disposition (*gotra; rigs*).
The spiritual affinity of an individual. It refers to natural affinity with a specific spiritual path and the potential to accomplish its result. According to the Yogācāra tradition there are five types of beings: those with a śrāvaka gotra, those with a pratyekabuddha gotra, those with a Mahayana gotra, those with an undefined gotra, and those with a cut-off gotra. According to Madhyamaka, this presentation is only an expedient means, as all beings eventually reach the perfect awakening of buddhahood.

ten powers (*daśa-bala; stobs bcu*).
Part of the qualities unique to a buddha. The ten powers are (1) the power of understanding proper and improper causes, (2) the power of understanding the outcome

of actions, (3) the power of understanding the various aspirations, (4) the power of understanding the various natural temperaments, (5) the power of understanding the various types of mental faculties, (6) the power of understanding the various paths leading to their corresponding destinations, (7) the power of knowing all the defiled and immaculate meditative concentrations, (8) the power of knowing prior births, (9) the power of knowing dying and rebirth, and (10) the power of knowing the exhaustion of defilements.

three natures (*trisvabhāva; ngo bo gsum*); also three characteristics (*trilakṣaṇa; mtshan nyid gsum*).
The model of reality according to the Yogācāra tradition, consisting of the imputed, the dependent, and the perfected. The imputed (*parikalpita; kun brtags*) is the erroneously imputed existence of apprehended objects and the apprehending mind as two separate entities; the dependent (*paratantra; gzhan dbang*) refers to all appearances or phenomena arising in dependence on causes and conditions; and the perfected (*pariniṣpanna; yongs grub*) refers to the realization of the true nature of appearances, that is, the dependent nature freed of the imputed duality. For a more detailed explanation see the introduction.

three vehicles (*triyāna; theg pa gsum*).
The three paths of liberation: the śrāvaka vehicle leading to the state of a śrāvaka arhat, the pratyekabuddha vehicle leading to the state of pratyekabuddha arhat, and the bodhisattva vehicle (Mahayana) leading to the state of complete awakening or buddhahood. According to the Cittamātra philosophy, these three vehicles are considered final in the sense that they each lead to their own final result. According to Madhyamaka, the first two are temporary vehicles for those with special affinity with those paths. Ultimately, however, all vehicles converge in the Mahayana, the path leading to perfect buddhahood.

total affliction (*saṃkleśa; kun nas nyon mongs pa*).
All dharmas belonging to samsara and its causes.

twelve branches of scripture (*dvādaśadharmapravacana; gsung rab kyi yan lag bcu gnyis*).
The twelve scriptural categories containing the Buddhist teachings: (1) discourses (*sūtra; mdo*), (2) melodic verses (*geya; dbyangs kyis bsnyad pa*), (3) prophecies and revelations (*vyākaraṇa; lung bstan pa*), (4) metered verses (*gāthā; tshig su bcad pa*), (5) special utterances (*udāna; ched du brjod pa*), (6) narratives (*nidāna; gleng gzhi*), (7) illustrative accounts (*avadāna; rtogs pa brjod pa*), (8) parables (*ityukta; de lta bu byung ba*), (9) past life accounts (*jātaka; skyes pa'i rabs*), (10) scriptures of great extent (*vaipulya; shin tu rgyas pa*), (11) marvelous accounts (*adbhutadharma; rmad du byung ba'i chos*), and (12) decisive teachings (*upadeśa; gtan la phab par bstan pa*).

two extremes (*antadvaya; mtha' gnyis*).

The distorted views of reality summarizing all types of wrong views. The two extremes are the view of permanence (*rtag pa'i lta ba*), which is the belief in an unchanging and independent essential nature, in particular in the individual; and the view of annihilation (*chad pa'i lta ba*), the belief that upon death every aspect of the individual is completely annihilated. The latter view has the implication of not believing in rebirth and the law of karma, deeds, and their results.

veil (*āvaraṇa; sgrib pa*).

That which impedes awakening. On the Mahayana path, two veils are removed: the veil of afflictions (*kleśāvaraṇa; nyon mongs pa'i sgrib pa*), consisting of the mental afflictions such as desire, anger, and so forth, and the cognitive veil (*jñeyāvaraṇa; shes bya'i sgrib pa*), consisting of the latencies and residues of the afflictions. By removing the first, one attains liberation from samsara, and by removing the second, the omniscient state of buddhahood.

Tibetan Names and Places with Transliteration and Notes

Name of person or place with dates, location, notes	Wylie transliteration
Chogye Trichen Khyenrab Lekshe Gyatso (1919–2007), former head of the Tsharpa subschool of the Sakya tradition	*bco brgyad khri chen mkhyen rab legs bshad rgya mtsho*
Dagpo Penchen Tashi Namgyal (1399–1458), master of the Dagpo Kagyü tradition	*dwags po paN chen bkra shis rnam rgyal*
Dolpopa Sherab Gyaltsen (1292–1361), founding master of the Jonang tradition	*dol po pa shes rab rgyal mtshan*
Drepung, Central Tibet, one of the three main monastic seats of the Gelug tradition	*'bras spungs*
Drogön Chögyal Phagpa (1235–1280), one of the five founding masters of the Sakya tradition	*'gro mgon chos rgyal 'phags pa*
Dzongpa Kunga Namgyal (1432–1496), founder of Gongkar Chöde monastery, seat of the Dzongpa subschool of the Sakya tradition	*dzong pa kun dga' rnam rgyal*
Ganden, Central Tibet, monastic seat of the Gelug tradition, founded by Tsongkhapa	*dga' ldan*
Gorampa Sönam Senge (1429–1489), Sakya master and important author, student of Rongtön	*go rams pa bsod nams seng ge*
Gö Lotsawa Zhönu Pel (1392–1481), Kagyü master and important author	*'gos lo tsA ba gzhon nu dpal*

Name of person or place with dates, location, notes	Wylie transliteration
Gyalmo Rong, Eastern Tibet, birth-place of Rongtön	*rgyal mo rong*
Jamgön Kongtrul Lodrö Thaye (1813–1899), Kagyü master of the Rimé nonsectarian movement	*'jam mgon kong sprul blo gros mtha' yas*
Jetsün Dragpa Gyaltsen (1147–1216), one of the five founding masters of the Sakya tradition	*rje btsun grags pa rgyal mtshan*
Jetsün Taranatha (1575–1634), master of the Jonang tradition	*rje btsun tA ra nA tha*
Ju Mipham (1846–1912), Nyingma master and important author	*'ju mi pham*
Khedrup Je Geleg Palsang (1385–1438), one of the principal disciples of Tsongkhapa	*mkhas grub dge legs dpal bzang*
Khenpo Appey Yönten Sangpo (1927–2010), recent master of the Sakya tradition	*mkhan po a pad yon tan bzang po*
Khenpo Shenga (1871–1927), Nyingma master and important author	*mkhan po gzhan dga'*
Khyenrab Chöje (1436–1497), Sakya master and abbot of Nālendra	*mkhyen rab chos rje*
Lhasa, Central Tibet, capital of Tibet	*lha sa*
Lopön Sönam Tsemo (1142–1182), one of five founding masters of the Sakya tradition	*slob dpon bsod nams brtse mo*
Müchen Sempa Chenpo Könchog Gyaltsen (1388–1469), one of the principal disciples of Ngorchen Kunga Sangpo	*mus chen sems dpa' chen po dkon mchog rgyal mtshan*

Name of person or place with dates, location, notes	Wylie transliteration
Nālendra, Central Tibet, monastic university in Phenyul established by Rongtön, named after the famous center of Buddhist studies in Northern India	nA len dra
Nedong, Central Tibet, Tibetan capital under the Phamo Drupa	sne gdong
Ngor, Central Tibet, main seat of the Ngor subschool of the Sakya tradition	ngor
Ngorchen Kunga Sangpo (1382–1456), founder of the Ngor subschool of the Sakya tradition	ngor chen kun dga' bzang po
Nyame Sherab Gyaltsen (1356–1415), master of the Bön tradition	mnyam med shes rab rgyal mtshan
Pang Lotsāwa Lodrö Tenpa (1276–1342), Sakya master and important author	dpang lo tsA ba blo gros bstan pa
Phadampa Sangye (d. 1117), Indian tantric master who taught in Tibet	pha dam pa sangs rgyas
Phamo Drupa, Tibetan dynasty that ruled Tibet in the fourteenth and fifteenth centuries	phag mo gru pa
Phenyul, Central Tibet, location of Nālendra monastery	'phan yul
Rangjung Dorje (1284–1339), the third Karmapa, head of the Karma Kagyü school	rang byung rdo rje
Rongtön Sheja Künrig (1367–1449), Sakya master and important author	rong ston shes bya kun rig
Sachen Kunga Nyingpo (1092–1158), one of the five founding masters of the Sakya tradition	sa chen kun dga' snying po

Name of person or place with dates, location, notes	Wylie transliteration
Sakya, Central Tibet, main seat of the Sakya tradition	*sa skya*
Sakya Pandita Kunga Gyaltsen (1182–1251), one of the five founding masters of the Sakya tradition	*sa skya paN Di ta kun dga' rgyal mtshan*
Sangphu Ne'uthog, Central Tibet, important monastic university	*gsang phu ne'u thog*
Sera, Central Tibet, one of the three main monastic seats of the Gelug tradition	*se ra*
Shakya Chokden (1428–1507), Sakya master and important author, student of Rongtön	*shA kya mchog ldan*
Thangtong Gyalpo (1361–1485), Tibetan yogi, architect, and civil engineer, famous for his longevity	*thang stong rgyal po*
Tsongkhapa Lobsang Dragpa (1357–1419), founder of the Gelug tradition	*tsong kha pa blo bzang grags pa*
Yaktön Sangye Pel (1348–1414), Sakya master and teacher of Rongtön	*g.yag ston sangs rgyas dpal*

BIBLIOGRAPHY

Bernert, Christian. "Rong-ston on Buddha-Nature: A Commentary on the Fourth Chapter of the Ratnagotravibhāga." Master's thesis, University of Vienna, 2009. (vv.1.27–95[a]).

Bhikkhu Bodhi, ed. *A Comprehensive Manual of Abhidhamma*. Charleston: Charleston Buddhist Fellowship, 2007.

Brunnhölzl, Karl. *The Center of the Sunlit Sky: Madhyamaka in the Kagyü Tradition*. Ithaca: Snow Lion Publications, 2004.

———. *Prajñāpāramitā, Indian "gzhan stong pas," and the Beginning of Tibetan gzhan ston*. Vienna: Arbeitskreis Fur Tibetische und Buddhistische Studien Universität Wien, 2011.

Chogay Trichen Rinpoche. *The History of the Sakya Tradition: A Feast for the Minds of the Fortunate* (Gangs-ljongs mdo-sngags kyi bstan-pa'i shing-rta dpal-ldan sa-skya-pa'i chos-'byung mdor-bsdus skal-bzang yid-kyi dga'-ston). Bristol: Ganesha Press, 1983.

D'Amato, Mario. *Maitreya's Distinguishing the Middle from the Extremes (Madhyāntavibhāga), along with Vasubandhu's Commentary (Madhyāntavibhāga-bhāṣya): A Study and Annotated Translation*. New York: American Institute of Buddhist Studies, 2012.

Dharmachakra Translation Committee. *Middle Beyond Extremes: Maitreya's Madhyantavibhaga with Commentaries by Khenpo Shenga and Ju Mipham*. Ithaca: Snow Lion Publications, 2006.

Jackson, David P. *The Early Abbots of 'Phan-po Nalendra: The Vicissitudes of a Great Tibetan Monastery in the 15th Century*. Vienna: Arbeitskreis für Tibetische und Buddhistische Studien, Universität Wien, 1989.

———. "Rong ston bKa' bcu pa. Notes on the title and travels of a great Tibetan scholastic." In *Pramāṇakīrtiḥ: Papers dedicated to Ernst Steinkellner on the occasion of his 70th birthday*, vol. 1, edited by Birgit Kellner, et al., 345–360. Wien: Arbeitskreis für Tibetische und Buddhistische Studien, Universität Wien, 2007.

———. *Rong-ston on the Prajñāpāramitā Philosophy of the Abhisamayālaṃkāra: His Subcommentary on Haribhadra's 'Sphuṭārthā.'* Kyoto: Nagata Bunshōdō, 1988.

Karma Choephel, David. *Jewels from the Treasury: Vasubandhu's Verses on the Treasury of Abhidharma and Its Commentary Youthful Play by the Ninth Karmapa Wangchuk Dorje*. Woodstock: KTD Publications, 2012.

Karma Phuntsho. *Mipham's Dialectics and the Debates on Emptiness: To Be, Not To Be or Neither*. London: Routledge, 2005.

Kobayashi, Mamoru. "The Madhyamaka Thought of Roṅ ston Śākya rgyal mtshan and Its Impact." In *Memoirs of the Research Department of the Toyo Bunko No. 63.* Tokyo: The Toyo Bunko, 2005.

Komarovski, Yaroslav. "Echoes of Empty Luminosity: Reevaluation and Unique Interpretation of Yogācāra and Niḥsvabhāvavāda Madhyamaka by the Fifteenth-Century Tibetan Thinker Śākya mchog ldan." PhD thesis, University of Virginia, 2007.

La Vallée Poussin, Louis de. *Abhidharmakośabhāṣyam, Volume 1.* Translated by Leo M. Pruden. Berkeley: Asian Humanities Press, 1991.

———, ed. *Madhyamakāvatāra par Candrakīrti.* Osnabrück: Biblio Verlag, 1970.

Lopez, Donald S. *The Heart Sutra Explained: Indian and Tibetan Commentaries.* Albany: SUNY Press, 1988.

Mathes, Klaus-Dieter. *Unterscheidung der Gegebenheiten von ihrem wahren Wesen* (Dharmadharmatāvibhāga). In *Indica et Tibetica* 26. Swisttal-Odendorf: Indica et Tibetica Verlag, 1996.

Mipham, Jamgon Ju. *Speech of Delight: Mipham's Commentary of Shantarakshita's Ornament of the Middle Way.* Translated by Thomas H. Doctor. Ithaca: Snow Lion Publications, 2004.

Nagao, Gadjin M., ed. *Madhyantavibhaga-bhasya: A Buddhist Philosophical Treatise Edited for the First Time from a Sanskrit Manuscript.* Tokyo: Suzuki Research Foundation, 1964.

Obermiller, Eugene. *The Jewelry of Scripture of Bu-ston.* Delhi: Sri Satguru, 1987.

Padmakara Translation Group, trans. *The Adornment of the Middle Way: Shantarakshita's Madhyamakalankara with Commentary by Jamgön Mipham.* Boston: Shambhala Publications, 2005.

Powers, John. *Wisdom of Buddha: The Saṁdhinirmocana Sūtra.* Berkeley: Dharma Publishing, 1995.

Rong ston rma ba'i seng ge. *dbus mtha' rnam 'byed dang chos dang chos nyid rnam 'byed rtsa 'grel.* Khreng tu'u (Chengdu): Si khron mi rigs dpe skrun khang, 1998.

Schmithausen, Lambert. "Ālayavijñāna. On the Origin and Early Development of a Central Concept of Yogācāra Philosophy," *Studia Philologica Buddhica Monograph Series,* vol. IV ab. Tokyo: International Institute for Buddhist Studies, 1987.

———. "On the Problem of the Relation of Spiritual Practice and Philosophical Theory in Buddhism." In *German Scholars on India. Contributions to Indian Studies,* vol. II. New Delhi: Nachiketa Publications Ltd., 1976, 235–50.

Stanley, Richard. "A Study of the *Madhyāntavibhāga-Bhaṣya-Tīkā.*" PhD thesis, Australian National University, 1988.

Stcherbatsky, Theodore. *Madhyanta-Vibhanga: Discourse on Discrimination between Middle and Extremes, ascribed to Bodhisattva Maitreya and commented by Vasubhandu and Sthiramathi, translated from the Sanscrit.* Moskow/Leningrad: Bibliotheca Buddhica XXX, Academy of Sciences USSR Press, 1936.

Stearns, Cyrus. *The Buddha from Dölpo. A Study of the Life and Thought of the Tibetan Master Dölpopa Sherab Gyaltsen.* Ithaca: Snow Lion Publications, 2010.

Thurman, Robert, ed. *The Universal Vehicle Discourse Literature (Mahāyā-nasūtrālaṃkāra) by Maitreyanātha/Āryāsaṅga, together with its Commentary (Bhāṣya) by Vasubandhu.* New York: American Institute of Buddhist Studies at Columbia University, 2004.

Waldron, William. *The Buddhist Unconscious. The Alayavijñāna in the Context of Indian Buddhist Thought.* New York: Routledge, 2003.

Wangchuk, Dorji. "On the Status of the Yogācāra School in Tibetan Buddhism." In *The Foundation for Yoga Practitioners: The Buddhist* Yogācārabhūmi *Treatise and Its Adaptation in India, East Asia, and Tibet,* edited by Ulrich Timme Kragh, 1316–1328. Harvard Oriental Series 75. Cambridge, MA: The Department of South Asian Studies, 2013.

Williams, Paul. *Mahāyāna Buddhism: The Doctrinal Foundations.* Second Edition. London and New York: Routledge, 2000.

Yamabe, Nobuyoshi. "Riposte." In *Pruning the Bodhi Tree. The Storm Over Critical Buddhism,* edited by Paul Loren Swanson and Jamie Hubbard. Honolulu: University of Hawai'i Press, 1997, 208–19.

INDEX

abandonment, path of, 87
abandonments, four perfect, 55, 77, 126n43
Abhidharma, 5, 15, 17
Abhidharmakośa (Vasubandhu), 52, 122n29, 126n33
Abhidharmasamuccaya (Asaṅga), 5, 122n29
Abhisamayālaṃkāra (Ornament of Clear Realization), 12, 17, 122n29
    commentaries on, 18, 122–23n45
abiding reality, 68, 69, 128n73
Acalā, 123n2
accomplishments, genuine, 103–4
accumulation, path of, 75–76, 84, 127n46, 130n98
accumulations, two, 48
actuality, unmistaken regarding, 96, 98
Adorning Maitreya's Intent
    conclusion and aspiration, 107–8
    editions of, 21
    greatness and necessity of, 104–5
    homage, 27–28
    title of, 29
adventitious, unmistaken regarding, 94, 97, 98, 131n112
afflictions, 130n91
    as adventitious, 45
    all-base consciousness and, 8
    five, 46, 125n20
    Madhyamaka view of, 11
    nine fetters of, 46–47
    origination and, 74
    in proving emptiness, 44–45
    qualities obstructed by, 47–48
    ultimate lack of, 97–98
    See also total affliction
agitation, 55, 78–79, 93, 110
Ajita (Maitreya), 27, 107, 124n3
all-base consciousness, 4
    affliction and, 38
    as appearances, 34
    as basis of mental engagement, 95
    bhavaṅga-citta and, 120n12

causal and resultant, 8
    as causal condition, 37
    latencies in, 65
    in Yogācāra, 7
analysis, 1, 9, 66, 77, 126n44. *See also* reasoning
anger, 14, 47, 56, 125n20, 125n26
antidotes, 15
    as eight formative factors, 110–11
    eighteen stages of, 83–85
    expertise in, 70–75
    extremes of conceptualizing, 102
    grounds as, 59
    to mistaken perceptions of reality, 63
    as obstruction to miraculous powers, 55
    path as, 66, 74
    of path of accumulation, 75–76
    purification by, 41, 45
    results based on, 85–87
    sequence of teaching, 31
    to ten views of self, 60
    three natures and, 70
appearances, 6, 8–9, 34, 35, 95–96
Appey Yonten Sangpo, Khenpo, 18, 124n5
apprehended and apprehender
    dependence between, 34, 124n5
    existence of nonexistence of, 13–14, 39–40, 125n15
    extremes of, 101, 102
    freedom from, 95, 96
    purification of, 43
    separation of, 36
    three natures in, 8–9, 34–35, 61–62, 66
apprehension, modes of, 36, 69–70, 124n70
arrogance, lack of, 94, 97, 99
āryas, dharmas of, 41, 125n16
Asaṅga, 4, 5, 11, 12, 13
ascetic practices, 47, 125n22
aspiration, pāramitā of, 57, 89, 90
attachment, 1, 46, 47–48, 50, 54
attention, mental factor of, 37, 131n106
awakening
    quality of, 51